TOP DOGS

True Stories of Canines That Made History

ELIZABETH MACLEOD

annick press

toronto + berkeley + vancouver

Cover art/design by Pixel Hive Studio
Edited by Chandra Wohleber
Cover art/design by Pixel Hive Studio
Designed by Pixel Hive Studio
Annick Press Ltd.

We acknowledge the support of the Canada Council for the Arts, the Ontario Arts Council, and the participation of the Government of Canada/la participation du gouvernement du Canada for our publishing activities.

Cataloging in Publication

MacLeod, Elizabeth, author

Top dogs : true stories of canines that made history / Elizabeth MacLeod.

Issued in print and print electronic formats.

ISBN 978-1-55451-907-1 (hardback).--ISBN 978-1-55451-906-4

(paperback).--ISBN 978-1-55451-909-5 (pdf).--ISBN 978-1-55451-908-8

(epub)

1. Working dogs--History--Juvenile literature. I. Title.

SF428.2.M32 2017   j636.7'0886   C2016-906258-9
                                               C2016-906259-7

Published in the U.S.A. by Annick Press (U.S.) Ltd.

Distributed in Canada by University of Toronto Press.

Distributed in the U.S.A. by Publishers Group West.

Printed in China

Visit us at: www.annickpress.com

Also available in e-book format. Please visit www.annickpress.com/ebooks.html for more details.
Or scan

CONTENTS

IN MEMORY OF Senator,
A DEAR LITTLE DOG,
AND WITH LOVE
TO HER FAMILY.

PAW PRINTS THROUGH HISTORY

Curled up on a lap, stretched out by their owners' feet, or trotting along for a walk—dogs are an important part of many people's lives. Experts say there are more than 525 million dogs in the world. About 75 million of them live in the United States—no other country has more pet dogs—and approximately 6 million pooches can be found in homes in Canada.

Dogs have lived side by side with humans for as many as 32,000 years. Scientists believe they were the first animal that ancient humans tamed or domesticated. These early pets helped their owners hunt, guarded their families, and, like today, were faithful companions.

Because dogs have lived with humans for a long time, they've learned to interpret human behavior and even to decode some facial expressions. And people have learned to decipher how their pet dogs are feeling, although sometimes we've needed a little help. In 2003, a scientist who specializes in canine behavior invented the "wagometer," a device that measures the wag of a dog's tail to interpret the mutt's mood.

But dogs are far more than pets— they've changed history too. In this book, you can find out about dogs that have rescued explorers. Some dogs have gone to war, serving on the battlefield or guarding military facilities. Dogs have even saved cities from deadly diseases by transporting medicine.

You can also read about search and rescue dogs that have pulled people out of collapsing buildings. Service dogs help their deaf or blind owners every day, comfort people suffering from post-traumatic stress disorder (PTSD), an anxiety disorder that a person can develop after he experiences a traumatic event, and sniff the breath of people with diabetes to alert them if their blood-sugar level is dropping. Some dogs assist those with autism.

Dogs are so important to people that lots of expressions include them. If you're not feeling well, you're "sick as a dog." If your feet hurt, you might say, "My dogs are barking!" Feeling really happy? Then you're "like a dog with two tails."

If you're having trouble learning a new skill, someone might say, "Well, you can't teach an old dog new tricks." Your parents might call your messy bedroom "a dog's breakfast" or say it's "gone to the dogs." To tidy it up, you may have to "work like a dog."

Hot diggity dog (that means "wow")— it's amazing how important dogs are to us!

CHAPTER 1
Seaman
the Newfoundland:
LEWIS AND CLARK'S
expedition
→ ACROSS
THE UNITED STATES
1804-1806

HANDING OVER HIS $20, Meriwether Lewis took the leash of the huge black dog. The Newfoundland trotted quietly at his side through the streets of Pittsburgh, Pennsylvania, immediately impressing Lewis with its intelligence.

Although Newfoundland dogs were rare in the United States in the early 1800s, Lewis knew these dogs were famous for their strength and ability to swim. Because of the dog's skills in the water, Lewis decided to call his new pet Seaman. On August 30, 1803, the pair left Pittsburgh and sailed to St. Louis, Missouri, to begin the adventure of their lives.

A Rather Large Purchase

Earlier that year, the United States had completed the Louisiana Purchase, in which they bought the Louisiana Territory from France. This vast swath included land in 15 present-day states from the Mississippi River to the Rocky Mountains. Little was known about the area's Native people, or about its wild animals, climate, soil, and plants. There were Native settlements, but no stores, doctors, or railways.

President Thomas Jefferson chose Lewis to lead an expedition across the new territory to discover and record what was there and create maps of the terrain. Lewis was 29 years old and a skilled hunter and outdoorsman. Lewis had experience negotiating with Native people and was a soldier and politician. In 1801, he had become an aide to Jefferson, managing his schedule and staff.

WOOf!

The $20 Lewis spent in 1803 to buy Seaman would be worth about $500 today.

When Meriwether Lewis was just a teenager, he went out hunting on mid-winter nights with his dogs.

The Louisiana Purchase was the United States' largest single land purchase.

Treaty
Between the United States of America and The French Republic

The President of the United States of America, and the First Consul of the French Republic in the name of the French People, desiring to remove all Source of misunderstanding relative to objects of discussion, mentioned in the second and fifth Articles of the Convention of the {8th Vendémiaire, an 9} {30 September 1800} relative to the rights claimed by the United States in virtue of the Treaty concluded

Fisherman's Friend

The Newfoundland dog was first bred more than 400 years ago from the St. John's dog, which is native to Newfoundland, and the Portuguese mastiff. They were used as working dogs by the people who fished the waters off the island of Newfoundland, on Canada's east coast. These large dogs pulled up fishing nets, and the biggest ones hauled carts and other equipment.

Newfoundlands are famous for rescuing fishermen and other people who fall into the ocean's icy waters. Their webbed feet make them great swimmers. They don't "dog paddle" like most dogs but move their paws to the side, like they are doing the breaststroke. Newfoundlands also seem to have an instinct for lifesaving and show great courage performing rescues.

The Corps of Discovery

Lewis called on his long-time friend William Clark, an army lieutenant with excellent wilderness survival skills, to lead the group with him. Clark hired and trained the crew, 33 men who were volunteers in the United States Army. They became known as the Corps of Discovery.

The men had no idea how long the expedition would take. The only thing they knew was that it would be risky trekking through unknown territory—with no roads and no maps—and would require all their strength and skill. Joining the Corps of Discovery were more than 200 dogs, but none would prove to be as valuable to the expedition as Seaman.

Lewis traveled to Philadelphia, Pennsylvania, to meet with Jefferson's scientist friends. They taught him to navigate and perform first aid. That training was supposed to help the men in his crew, but it would also end up saving Seaman's life.

The Dog Is Not for Sale!

The expedition was scheduled to depart in spring 1804 from near St. Louis, Missouri, so Lewis and Seaman headed down the Ohio River to meet up with the other men. The captain discovered that Seaman was extremely good at catching squirrels, and in mid-September, Lewis wrote in his journal, "I made my dog take as many each day as I had occasion for."

Two months later, Lewis and Seaman reached the area where the Ohio and Mississippi Rivers meet, probably somewhere in the present state of Illinois. They met with a group of Shawnee Native people who tried to trade three beaver skins for the great black beast. But Seaman had already impressed Lewis with his loyalty and smarts, and Lewis refused to part with the dog, writing in his journal, "of course there was no bargain."

During the Lewis and Clark expedition, William Clark's main jobs were to manage the supplies, lead hunting expeditions, and draw maps.

Heading into the Wilderness

Preparations for the expedition continued, and on May 14, 1804, the men began their journey from near St. Louis. They paddled northwest up the Missouri River. Seaman padded along the riverbank beside the boats or rode with Lewis in one of the crafts. At night, when the expedition camped onshore, Seaman wandered off and explored on his own. Lewis was always relieved when his dog returned.

At first, the men who wrote about Seaman in their journals called him "the dog" or "Captain Lewis's dog." But he was a good companion and very helpful at catching animals for food. On July 15, 1806, Lewis recorded that "Seaman . . . proves his worth by brining down an Elk calf." Soon all the men were calling him "our dog."

When Seaman was in one of the expedition's boats, he tried to stay near Lewis.

Rescue Heroes

In 1995, a Newfoundland dog named Boo pulled a man from the Yuba River in California. The man was hearing impaired and mute, so he couldn't call for help. Without Boo's aid, he would likely have drowned.

Bilbo the Newfoundland was a beach-rescue dog in Cornwall, England, and Britain's most famous lifesaving dog. He saved three lives and kept tourists from wading into the sea when the currents were too strong.

In New Jersey, in February 1983, a Newfoundland called Villa heard the cries of a 12-year-old neighbor trapped in a snowbank. Villa jumped a fence and then circled the girl to clear the snow around her. The dog positioned herself so the girl could grab her and be hauled out of the snowdrift.

A Near-Fatal Bite

At the end of October, the group built Fort Mandan, in North Dakota, and spent the winter there. It was too cold and snowy to continue the exploration safely, so they spent the time repairing equipment, drying meat, and making clothes from animal skins. In April 1805, they continued their trek west to the coast. To help them communicate with the Native people, they were accompanied by Sacagawea, a Shoshone Indian woman.

The expedition often went hungry, so on May 19, the men were pleased when one of the corps members shot a beaver (above right)—the large animal would provide lots of meat to roast over the fire that night. But their delight turned to horror when Seaman swam out to retrieve the animal. When the big dog got close, the beaver—which was not yet dead—bit him in the hind leg, cutting through an artery (a tube that carries large amounts of blood from your heart to the rest of your body).

As the men carried Seaman back to camp, the bite was bleeding so badly Lewis was terrified his beloved dog would die. But thanks to the first aid Lewis had been taught, Seaman pulled through and was soon back to guarding the men and helping them hunt.

Seaman vs. the Wild Buffalo

It was a good thing they had saved Seaman because just 10 days later, on May 29, a large male buffalo stampeded through the camp. Seaman raced out, attacking the animal as it headed for the tent where Lewis and Clark were sleeping. Thanks to the dog's barking and nipping, the buffalo headed off into the night again, causing little damage. Seaman had saved the expedition!

Less than a month later, a bear barged through the woods near the camp. Although it ate some of the food for the expedition, Seaman's barking kept it away from the men.

Clark drew this picture of a sage-grouse in his journal.

WOOF!

Many explorers took Newfoundland dogs with them, including Sir John Franklin when he searched the Arctic for the Northwest Passage in the mid-1800s.

THE First Dog

The earliest dog ancestor on earth looked a lot like a weasel: about 40 million years ago, this little creature, called *Miacis*, lived in trees.

It evolved into *Tomarctus* approximately 23 million years ago. A sharp-nosed furry animal, *Tomarctus* was only about 46 centimeters (18 inches) high. It was the ancestor to wolves and jackals, as well as dogs.

About 35,000 years ago, dogs evolved to be separate from wolves. Scientists have found evidence that people began taming dogs around 32,000 years ago.

Ancient peoples must have appreciated dogs' keen sense of smell, which helped them track down dinner, as well as their sharp teeth to guard against enemies and more dangerous wild animals. Dogs surely appreciated people sharing food!

The first identifiable dog breed, a type of greyhound, appeared about 9000 BCE, recorded in Egyptian paintings and carvings. This tall, slim dog was trained by the ancient Egyptians to help them hunt. Other ancient breeds include the malamute, saluki, shar-pei, and shih tzu.

Salukis are graceful, intelligent dogs.

Bugs, Barbs, Bears, and Birds

Earlier that summer, Lewis wrote in his journal, "The musquetoes continue to infest us in such manner that we can scarcely exist . . . my dog even howls with the torture he experiences from them, they are almost insupportable, they are so numerous that we frequently get them in our throats as we breathe."

Another problem for Seaman, and for the entire corps, was needle-and-thread grass, which grew widely across the territory. Its barbed seeds pierced the men's moccasins and leggings. The seeds also clung to Seaman's heavy coat and, as Lewis recorded on July 26, 1805, "My poor dog suffers with them excessively."

The bristle on each seed of needle-and-thread grass helps the seed twist and drill its way into the ground.

Seaman was a fast learner. He watched and copied how wolves and bears took advantage of antelopes' weak swimming to catch and eat them. Seaman would dive into a river or lake, swim up to one of these deer-like animals, bite the back of its neck, push it underwater to drown it, then tow it back to the waiting men. Seaman also learned to hunt wild geese.

Seaman Reaches the Pacific

On August 17, 1805, the expedition stood on the Continental Divide, the place in the Rocky Mountains where the streams on the eastern side all flow into the Gulf of Mexico and the Atlantic Ocean, while the waters on the western side flow toward the Pacific Ocean.

A few months later, in November 1805, they reached the Pacific Coast at the mouth of the Columbia River. Seaman must have stood with the men as they stared out over the vast ocean and heard the

WOOF!

You can read about Lewis and Clark's adventures in their own words online: lewisandclarkjournals. unl.edu

Gander THE Hero

Pal was a pet Newfoundland given to a regiment of the Canadian Army during World War II. At that time, the soldiers were stationed at Gander International Airport in Newfoundland, so they renamed the dog Gander.

The regiment sailed to Hong Kong in 1941 and Gander went too. During the Battle of Hong Kong, which began on December 8, 1941, the brave Newfoundland chased Japanese invaders away from wounded Canadians.

When Japanese soldiers threw a grenade at the Canadian soldiers, Gander picked up the bomb in his mouth and raced with it toward the enemy. He saved the lives of many Canadians, but sadly was killed when the grenade exploded.

Gander with members of the Royal Rifles of Canada in Hong Kong

EMPEROR'S Savior

Napoleon Bonaparte (below), emperor of France in the early 1800s, led his country into many battles, winning most of them. However, in 1812, Napoleon began losing major battles and was exiled by other European countries to the island of Elba in the Mediterranean Sea. It wasn't long before he began planning his escape.

On February 26, 1815, Napoleon was in a fisherman's boat, desperately making his way through the choppy seas to mainland France. Suddenly, a huge wave pitched him overboard! The fisherman's Newfoundland dog jumped into the rough waters and kept the emperor afloat until he could reach safety. When he got back in France, his army went to battle again—but Napoleon ended up being exiled once more!

Sacagawea (right), a Shoshone woman, was vital to Lewis and Clark's expedition.

waves crash against the rocky shore. The men spent the winter near the coast, building a base they called Fort Clatsop, after the Native people who lived in the area.

Dognapped!

In March 1806, the expedition headed home. They had survived attacks by animals, desperate hunger, and overturned boats. But for Lewis, the worst was yet to come.

On the night of April 11, Lewis was heartbroken to discover his dog had disappeared. But when the captain learned from a Clahclellah Native chief that three Watlala Native men had stolen Seaman, he was furious. He immediately sent three corpsmen after the thieves. As soon as the thieves realized Lewis's men were pursuing them, they let Seaman go and he bounded back to his friends.

Mission Accomplished

The expedition finally returned to St. Louis on September 23, 1806. Lewis and Clark had led the first official expedition to cross the United States from the Missouri River to the Pacific Ocean. They became two of the most famous explorers in American history.

The Corps of Discovery had covered more than 12,875 kilometers (8,000 miles). They met Native American tribes that Americans back east didn't even know existed. The men were also the first non–Native Americans to describe more than 300 animals and plants, including the grizzly bear, whooping crane, and wolverine.

Seaman was the only animal to complete the entire trip. He proved himself to be a strong, smart, loyal member of the expedition.

The big black Newfoundland remained with Lewis to the end. When the captain died on October 11, 1809, Seaman would not abandon him. Seaman even sat by Lewis's grave, refusing to eat. He pined away and died of grief on his master's grave.

WOOF!

Seaman's Day is celebrated with storytelling and crafts every July at Fort Clatsop, Oregon. The expedition stayed there in winter 1805/1806.

Non-Native Americans had never seen buffalo before the Lewis and Clark expedition.

There are many pictures and statues of Lewis and his brave dog Seaman.

CHAPTER 2
Lion Dogs:
CHINA'S
Boxer REBELLION

1899-1901

IT WAS THE EARLY EIGHTH CENTURY CE. Chinese emperor Ming's chess game was going badly. He was playing one of his princes, who'd been showing a little too much ambition for the emperor's liking. Members of the royal court had gathered to watch the match. It looked more and more certain that the prince would win, and the emperor was becoming upset.

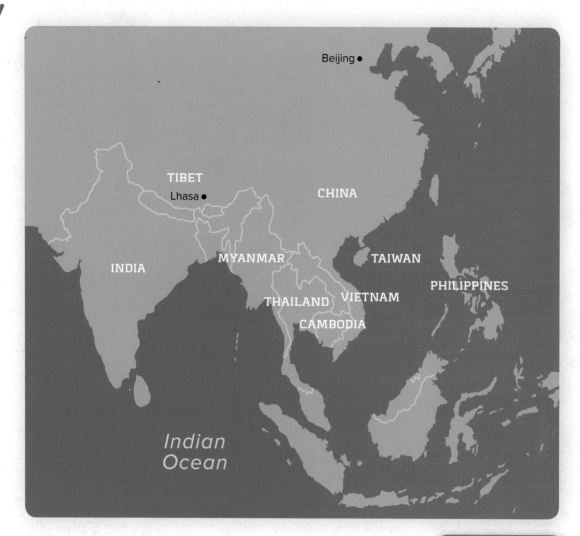

If he lost, the emperor would seem weak and the prince would gain more influence.

Carefully watching her master was the emperor's Pekingese, Wo. She hated to see him distressed. As the chess game continued, Wo couldn't stand her master's unhappiness any longer. She tried to jump into his arms but missed. Instead, she landed on the chessboard, scattering the pieces and ending the game.

The emperor apologized to the prince that they couldn't finish the match—but he was grinning as he spoke. And a few days later, little Wo was wearing a brand-new bejeweled collar ...

WOOF!

Because of their flat faces and noses, Pekingese can have trouble breathing in very hot or cold weather. They may also snore loudly!

This palace by the lake was one of Pekingese-loving Empress Dowager Cixi's (see page 19) favorite places.

Royal Canines

Pekingese have had a long history with Chinese royalty. They lived pampered lives as some of the most important members of the court beginning as long as 2,500 years ago. They snoozed in marble kennels lined with silk cushions. They ate only the best cuts of meat and had a team of staff to feed and groom them.

Their name comes from the city of Peking, now known as Beijing. The dogs lived with the royal court in a vast palace complex of nearly 1,000 buildings called the Forbidden City in Beijing's center.

The Lion of Buddha

About 2,000 years ago, traders from India brought the religion and philosophy of Buddhism to China. The practice follows the teachings of the Buddha (a holy man who lived in Nepal sometime between the sixth and the fourth century BCE) and encourages people to overcome greed, hatred, and ignorance and to try to end suffering for everyone.

Buddhism became popular in China, including with the royalty, but there was one big problem. Stories of the Buddha included a lion, which he tamed and adopted as his faithful servant and protector. But there were no lions in China, so this powerful religious symbol was missing. What could Chinese Buddhists do?

Someone looked at the dogs owned by the emperor and decided they resembled the carved statues of lions that had been brought to China. (In fact, these carvings didn't look much like real lions but instead had flattened faces, just like the Pekingese.) Because of this, the Pekingese became identified with the lion and were even more revered than they already had been.

In this statue of the Buddha, the hand held up is a symbol for the Buddha giving confidence or fearlessness.

THE Forbidden CITY

The palace complex where the Pekingese lived is called the Forbidden City (see below) because of an order that no one could enter or leave without the emperor's permission. It has about 980 buildings and is located in the center of Beijing. The Chinese royal family lived there from 1420 to 1912.

The Forbidden City was declared a World Heritage Site in 1987. It includes the world's largest grouping of ancient preserved wooden structures. The Palace Museum contains more than a million priceless works of art. About 15 million tourists visit the Forbidden City yearly, making it one of the most popular sites in the world.

Pekingese are known as toy dogs. In the past, they were kept to show wealth—or to attract fleas away from the owner!

VIP—Very Important Pooch

The royal court began to breed dogs that looked like this strange image of a lion. The most prized Pekingese were the ones with lots of fur around the face (like a mane), as well as wide noses and flattened faces. They became known as Lion Dogs.

The dogs were sacred symbols that only royalty could own. Removing one from the Forbidden City meant the death penalty. Toward the end of the second century CE, the emperor even made one of his dogs a member of the nobility. That put a Lion Dog above the advisers and aides, who were very insulted. It also started a trend of giving royal dogs special privileges, such as pensions for life!

Fortune-Telling Fidos

The Pekingese, or Pekes, were popular with Chinese royalty for centuries. If commoners encountered one, they had to look away, just as they did when they saw a royal or noble person. By the 1500s, they could only be bred within the Forbidden City, so they disappeared from the sight of commoners.

In the mid-1800s, Empress Dowager Cixi had more than 100 of them. She got her royal title when her husband, the emperor, died and it gave her power to rule until their young son was old enough to take over. But she craved more power. She felt being seen often with Pekingese would make her seem more important, thanks to the dogs' sacred, royal connection.

Cixi believed omens and signs could predict events and thought the Lion Dogs could foretell the future. Their colors and markings were used by her priests and fortune-tellers to make predictions. The birth of a yellow dog meant royalty and was also associated with the direction east. A red Pekingese foretold success and happiness.

Dogs with more than one color were called flowered, and the color patterns were thought to have special meanings. It was also believed that the number of puppies in a litter, the order in which they were born, and their genders foretold the future.

WOOf!

The Pekeatese is the result of mating a Pekingese with a Maltese. If you cross a Pekingese with a poodle, you get a Peekapoo!

Empress Dowager CiXi controlled the Chinese government from 1861 until she died in 1908. Unlike many of the women in the royal court, she could read and write.

Dog DATA

Why Dogs Make Good Pets

Loyal, smart, affectionate—no wonder dogs are one of the most popular pets in the world. Because they were the first animal that ancient peoples domesticated, or tamed, pooches have lived with people for a long time. That's allowed them to become very aware of what humans do and need. These pets have learned to understand and react to people's body language. Dogs also understand commands spoken to them.

Dogs are pack animals, which means they like to live in a group. A dog's owners become its pack, and canines are loyal to and protective of their pack. Living in a pack means dogs have to get along with the other members, and to do that, they have to communicate and be aware of moods and behaviors. This is why many dogs are so easy to train and can fit into a family's lifestyle.

Owning a dog can be good for you too. Walking your pet helps keep you healthy. The enthusiastic welcome she gives you, as well as the loving licks, can also make you feel better.

Sleeve Pekingese were likely used as hand warmers. They could also be fierce guard dogs.

What Does the Peke Say?

By the late 1800s, there were tensions in China. Cixi's son had died, and some people, like the current emperor (Cixi's nephew) wanted to modernize the country and bring in ideas from other nations. He ordered railways to be built and the military updated. Others, such as Cixi, wanted things to stay as they were and thought the influence of other countries would weaken Chinese culture.

People who supported Cixi encouraged her to get rid of her nephew, the emperor. What should she do? Of course, she consulted her beloved Lion Dogs. One of her favorites had just given birth to a yellow female, and Cixi took this to mean that she would be the sole ruler of China. She got right to work on a plan to make this happen.

Sleeve Pekingese

Can you imagine a dog small enough to fit in your sleeve? Pekingese come in different types, and the smallest is known as the sleeve Pekingese. During the Tang Dynasty (618–907 CE), the Chinese Imperial Household began to breed Pekingese small enough to fit in the billowing sleeves of their silk robes.

The small dogs gave the owners companionship and warmth. Today, sleeve Pekingese weigh no more than 2.7 kilograms (6 pounds). Slightly larger dogs are called mini-Pekingese. Some "sleeves" are as small as 1.4 kilograms (3 pounds) but are surprisingly strong with lots of energy.

TEMPLE DOGS

High in the mountains of Tibet, the Lhasa apso was bred to help guard Buddhist temples, or monasteries, and the monks who lived in them. Lhasa is the capital city of Tibet and apso is a Tibetan word that means "bearded." But thousands of years ago, they were known in Tibet as Apso Seng Kyi, which means "Bearded Lion Dog."

Guarding a temple's outermost doors were large Tibetan mastiffs (below). These dogs can stand as tall as 84 centimeters (33 inches). But if intruders managed to sneak past them, the Lhasa apsos were ready to bark a loud warning.

Since they were bred as watchdogs, Lhasas have excellent hearing. They are suspicious of strangers but loyal to their owners. These dogs are one of the oldest breeds in the world—scientists believe they were bred as early as 800 BCE.

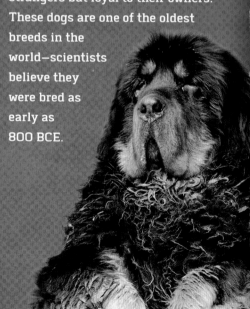

Boxers got their name because they practiced martial arts to stay fit.

The Boxers

Cixi's troops imprisoned the emperor in a palace in the middle of a lake in the Forbidden City. Success! But soon, Cixi had more decisions to make. A violent secret society, known as the Righteous and Harmonious Fists, or Boxers, felt the foreign businesses and Christian missionaries in China were bad for the country. They wanted them gone and didn't care how violently they had to fight to make them go.

Some members of the royal court supported the Boxers. Cixi wondered if she should support them too. Again, she consulted her Pekingese. Her dog Flowery-Duck had just given birth to three pups. Two were red, meaning success, and one was yellow, for royalty. Cixi felt she had her answer.

The End of the Lion Dogs?

The Boxer Rebellion began in 1899, pitting the Boxers against foreigners in many parts of China. It was successful at first for Cixi and her fighters. But the Boxers killed so many foreigners that soon their countries got involved. Americans, British, French, Germans, and Japanese marched on Beijing. In August 1900, they captured it and stormed the Forbidden City.

Cixi disguised herself as a peasant and barely escaped. She had already had her favorite Pekes carried away. But there wasn't enough time to save all the Lion Dogs. Rather than let them fall into foreign hands, she commanded that none of the remaining dogs be left alive.

Change Comes to China

The Boxer Rebellion ended in 1900 with the defeat of Cixi's forces. She was allowed to return to the Forbidden City, and she now favored the building of railways and many other foreign cultural and technological changes, including modern schools and a more just legal system.

Lion dogs were still considered too special for commoners, but Cixi gave some of her dogs to a few notable foreigners, including the daughter of American president Theodore Roosevelt. When Cixi died in 1908, her elaborate funeral included a chief priest carrying her favorite Lion Dog, Peony.

THE Year OF THE DOG

Do you know anyone born in 2006? You might say that person is a dog! According to the traditional Chinese calendar, the years roll by in a 12-year cycle. Each of those years is represented by an animal, such as the tiger, monkey, horse—or dog.

People born in 2006, 1994, and 1982 are said to act like dogs. They are honest and loyal, as well as stubborn and uncomfortable in crowds. "Dogs" are best suited to careers like judge, scientist, or nurse. Like real dogs, people born in the Year of the Dog will do anything for people who are important to them.

Pekingese Back in Power

The Communist Party came into power in China in the mid-1900s, insisting that all wealth should be shared. Rich people were seen as corrupt because it was felt they must have taken advantage of others to accumulate their wealth. Many wealthy people had owned Pekingese, which were confiscated by the Communists. The dogs almost disappeared from China.

Today, you can see Pekingese in China, many of them bred in the late 1900s from the dogs that were taken away or given as presents. These smart but stubborn dogs are excellent watchdogs and will bravely defend their owners. In ancient times, commoners had to bow down to the Lion Dogs—and some owners say the little dogs still expect to be treated that way!

CHAPTER 3

Combat CANINE:

WORLD WAR I's brave dog soldier

1914-1918

"SCRAM, YA MANGY MUTT!"
The little stray gave a doggy grin, then trotted away with his short tail wagging. He couldn't coax a snack from that cook, but here at the American army training camp, there were plenty of soldiers, and that meant lots of cooks. He'd just keep trying.

This thin brown-and-white dog was barely as tall as the soldiers' knees. Hardly the kind of heroic canine that helps win a war. So when he wandered into that camp at Yale University in New Haven, Connecticut, in July 1917, no one imagined he'd become World War I's most famous dog.

Messenger dogs were very loyal to two masters and would carry messages quickly between both.

CANADA

UNITED STATES
• Washington, D.C.
• New Haven

Atlantic Ocean

GREAT BRITAIN

GERMANY

Paris • • Seicheprey
• Marcheville
FRANCE

PORTUGAL SPAIN

ITALY

Thanks to his short legs and tail, he earned the name Stubby. He was probably a Boston terrier, a breed that's easy to train, friendly, and stubborn.

Stubby especially seemed to like men in uniform—although only American uniforms, as he would later show. It wasn't long before the little mutt had picked out his favorite soldier, James Robert Conroy of the 102nd infantry, Yankee Division.

The War Begins

Conroy and the other soldiers were training to fight in World War I. On one side were the Central Powers, including Austria–Hungary, Germany, and Turkey. Battling them were the Allies, with such countries as France, Russia, and Great Britain along with its commonwealth countries, including Canada and Australia.

The United States stayed out of the battle at first. But then, German submarines began sinking American ships. On April 6, 1917, the United States joined the Allies.

Soldiers (and Dogs!) in Training

Private James Conroy was taught how to march, dig trenches, and attack with bayonets. It was probably Conroy who taught Stubby to stand up and solemnly raise his right paw to the right side of his face in a salute. Little did Stubby or Conroy know how important this would become.

In September 1917, Conroy's regiment left New Haven, headed for battle in Europe. Conroy stealthily smuggled Stubby on board their ship. When they arrived in France in early October 1917, Conroy hid the pooch under his heavy coat and snuck him onto land.

James Conroy was proud to have his photograph taken with his clever, loyal dog, Stubby. They helped each other survive World War I.

Gas masks looked strange but saved the lives of many soldiers—and dogs.

But soon after arriving, Conroy's commanding officer found out about Stubby. The soldier and his dog were called before the furious commander.

Conroy waited nervously. However, before the officer could say a word, Stubby stood up and smartly saluted him. The little stray was immediately named the regiment's mascot and Conroy escaped punishment. Stubby had saved the day!

Death on the Wind

In early February 1918, Conroy's regiment moved closer to the combat zone. The soldiers and Stubby were stationed in a series of trenches northeast of Paris. Trenches, little more than deep ditches, gave the soldiers some cover from gunfire but were wet, cold, smelly, and full of lice and rats. The men often went hungry when supplies couldn't reach them. But there was worse to come.

On March 17, artillery shells containing poison gas rained down on the soldiers, burning their eyes and throats. World War I was the first war in which poison gases ("chemical weapons") were used. Choking and hacking, the soldiers struggled to slip on gas masks—and to put one on Stubby. Conroy had had a dog-sized mask specially made.

Stubby was likely a Boston terrier. This breed is known as the American gentleman because its white chest looks like a tuxedo shirt.

Messenger
Mutt

Another dog famous in World War I was Rags. The fluffy mixed-breed terrier was discovered by an American soldier on the streets of Paris. Rags became the mascot for the soldier's division but was even more useful. Messages written on paper were tucked into his collar, and he ran them from headquarters to the front lines.

Rags delivered his messages despite being bombed, gassed, and partially blinded. He could also sense, long before the men, when they were about to be bombed and would drop to the ground with his paws spread out. The men learned to watch him for an early warning.

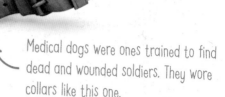

Medical dogs were ones trained to find dead and wounded soldiers. They wore collars like this one.

Thanks to Stubby's keen sense of smell, he could sense a gas attack long before the soldiers did. When he sensed the dangerous odors, Stubby would race through the trenches, yelping and even waking sleeping fighters by nipping at them. Stubby's bark-warning helped save a French town from a poison gas attack, and the village's grateful women sewed him a little jacket.

Jobs for Dogs

Stubby wasn't the first dog to accompany military divisions. Dogs had been joining soldiers at war both officially and unofficially for hundreds of years. Stubby and other dogs raised the soldiers' spirits by keeping them company on watch and snuggling with them when they slept.

On the battlefields, dogs also pulled cannons, supply wagons, and carts full of wounded soldiers. Dogs killed the rats that stole food and ran over the soldiers' bodies as they slept. A dog called Philly was a mascot and watchdog for another company of American soldiers. She was such a good guard that the Germans put a bounty on her!

With a message tied to its collar, this dog leaps over a trench and races off.

Wounded in Action

In April 1918, during the Battle of Seicheprey in northeast France, a shell exploded near Stubby, ripping open his chest and left front leg. The little dog howled in pain, and Conroy rushed him to a first-aid station.

Although many soldiers were there who needed help, a doctor took time to examine Stubby. He was badly hurt, but the doctor thought Stubby might pull through if he got immediate attention. The wounded animal was placed in an ambulance and rushed to a field hospital.

Surgeons carefully stitched up Stubby's injuries. It took him six weeks to recover, but soon he was back in the trenches with Conroy.

Stubby to the Rescue!

Now Stubby also became a rescue dog, locating wounded men in no-man's-land, the dangerous exposed area between the two sides' trench systems—close to enemy lines and full of thick mud as well as deep craters.

WOOF!

Other animals that served in World War I included carrier pigeons, horses, cats, camels, and even slugs—they shrink when exposed to even small amounts of mustard gas, warning nearby soldiers.

Many dogs aided troops on both sides of the battles in World War I by helping to rescue wounded soldiers.

PRISONER-OF-WAR DOG

Judy, a purebred pointer, was a mascot for a British navy ship stationed in China during World War II. She alerted the crew to pirates and enemy aircraft.

During the Battle of Singapore in 1942, the ship sank. Judy and the crew escaped to a deserted island. By finding drinking water, Judy saved the crew's lives.

A few weeks later, the crew were taken prisoner by Japanese soldiers. Judy is the only animal that was a registered Japanese prisoner of war in World War II. She caught snakes and rats for the starving men—and herself—to eat. Judy survived the war and was smuggled back to Britain. She won the Dickin Medal, an award for brave animals.

Judy was a smart dog who even survived an attack by a crocodile.

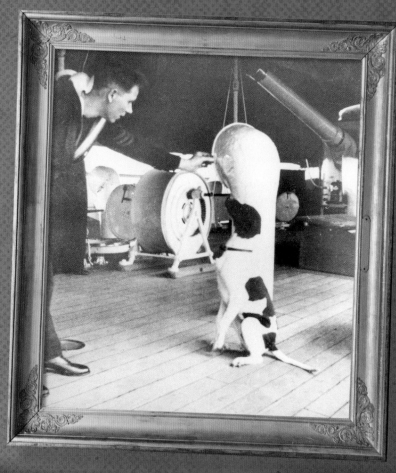

But Stubby scampered easily over the rough ground. With his keen nose, he could locate soldiers, even those almost buried in the heavy muck. Stubby would stay with the injured soldier and bark for help. Or he'd race off to fetch a doctor. Then Stubby would begin looking for the next man to assist.

Dogs of War

As long ago as 4000 BCE, Egyptians, Chinese, Greeks, Persians, and ancient Britons used dogs to guard their camps and scout out enemies. Large dogs wearing spiked collars attacked and chased enemy soldiers.

In the 1500s, Great Danes and mastiffs wore armor into battle. Two hundred years later, dogs were used as messengers in Europe's Seven Years' War. Dogs guarded and tracked enemy soldiers in World War II. During the Cold War, from about 1947 to 1991, sentry dogs guarded nuclear weapons in the United States.

Dogs are still used in battle (see page 71). They can stop prisoners from escaping, or search areas too dangerous for humans to investigate. They can also detect ambushes and locate weapons. They may even wear vests fitted with cameras and microphones to send information back to the authorities.

For a long time, the most common war dog was the German shepherd. Now armies use smaller dogs with even better senses of smell, such as Belgian Malinois and Dutch shepherds.

Dogs' playfulness, loyalty, and love raise soldiers' spirits. A canine companion can also help soldiers suffering from post-traumatic stress disorder (PTSD) by loving, trusting, and protecting them.

Service dogs help soldiers with post-traumatic stress disorder (PTSD) carry out their daily activities.

WORLD WAR II'S
top DOG

One of the medals on Stubby's jacket is the World War I Victory Medal. It was awarded for military service between April 6, 1918 and November 11, 1918.

It's hard to believe a family pet from Pleasantville, New York, could become the most awarded dog in World War II. But it happened to Chips, a German shepherd–collie–Siberian husky mix.

This smart, easily trained dog guarded tanks for the American army in Europe and North Africa. Chips also once carried phone cable wires from a group of soldiers back to base so they could call for help.

He was most famous for attacking a nest of Italian gunners in 1943. (Italy was fighting alongside Germany at this point.) He was wounded but forced the soldiers to surrender.

Later that day, Chips helped take 10 more enemy soldiers prisoner. He survived the war and returned to the States.

Like most rescue dogs, Stubby learned to tell the difference between American soldiers and the enemy. Perhaps the enemy soldiers smelled strange to the little dog, due to the different food they ate, or their language may have sounded different to his sensitive ears.

Stubby saved many lives as a rescue dog. But one day, he showed even greater courage.

Sergeant Stubby

On September 26, 1918, Conroy's regiment was fighting near the medieval town of Marchéville in north-central France. When Stubby discovered a German soldier, he jumped into action. Howling and barking, the heroic pup raced after the fleeing enemy through the mud and torn-up fields.

Stubby chased his captive back toward the American lines. The German was about to escape when the canine soldier leapt and knocked him down. With his teeth clamped on the seat of the enemy's pants, Stubby stood guard until American soldiers arrived. Thanks to this accomplishment, Stubby received a new nickname: Sergeant Stubby.

Peace at Last

World War I ended when an armistice (a contract to end the fighting) was signed by the Central Powers and the Allies on November 11, 1918. On March 31, 1919, Conroy and Stubby were homeward bound. This time, the pooch didn't have to be smuggled onto the ship. Everyone was glad to have such a famous dog on board.

The regiment's ship arrived in Boston on April 7, 1919. Throughout the war, journalists and reporters had sent home stories of Stubby's incredible exploits. He was treated like a hero and marched in a place of honor in parades held to celebrate the soldiers.

WOOF!

In 1921, Stubby received a medal from General John J. Pershing, the top American commander in World War I.

People back in the United States were ecstatic when World War I ended. So was Conroy—he and Stubby could finally go home.

Stubby had a special harness that could hold an American flag.

From Battlefields to Football Fields

In the fall of 1921, Conroy began studying law at Georgetown University in Washington, D.C., and Stubby became the mascot for the school's football team. During halftime, he trotted onto the field to chase a football or butt it with his head.

The crowds loved Stubby's stunts—he often got more cheers than the football teams! Some people claim it was his romping that inspired the modern idea of the halftime show.

Stubby continued to win medals and impress fans across America. He even visited the White House twice.

Farewell to a Hero

Stubby died on March 16, 1926, cradled in Conroy's arms. Obituaries for Stubby appeared in newspapers across the country.

Conroy was determined Stubby would never be forgotten. A taxidermist preserved the dog's body, and Stubby was placed at the American Red Cross Museum in Washington until 1941, when the museum needed the space. Conroy kept Stubby for a time, and then, in 1956, Stubby became part of a display at the Smithsonian Institution. You can still find him there, along with his jacket and other memorabilia. Conroy lived until 1987.

Stubby has been called the dog that won the most medals in World War I.

FLYING Fido

An abandoned German shepherd puppy called Antis became a good-luck charm for a British air force squadron in World War II. Antis flew with his Czechoslovakian owner on more than 30 missions, calmly dozing while the plane soared and swooped.

Despite being blasted by antiaircraft fire, none of the planes in the group was shot down or even hit. No wonder the flyers felt Antis brought good luck.

Thanks to his sharp hearing and sense of smell, Antis found survivors who had been covered in rubble in bombing raids.

CHAPTER 4

Togo & Balto:

LIFESAVING SLED-DOG run in Alaska

1925

IN JANUARY 1925, THE CITY OF NOME, ALASKA, was in terrible trouble. Diphtheria, an extremely contagious infection causing high fever and even death, especially in children, was threatening to spread across Alaska's northern villages. This was in the days before vaccinations against the disease, and Nome had run out of the antitoxin serum that could act as a cure.

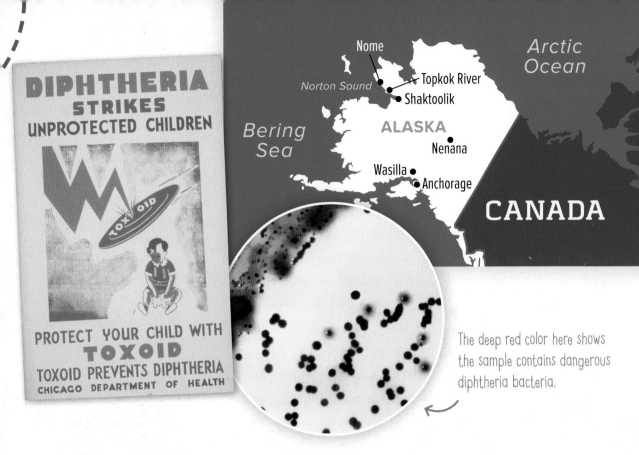

DIPHTHERIA STRIKES UNPROTECTED CHILDREN

PROTECT YOUR CHILD WITH TOXOID

TOXOID PREVENTS DIPHTHERIA
CHICAGO DEPARTMENT OF HEALTH

The deep red color here shows the sample contains dangerous diphtheria bacteria.

A desperate plea for the serum went out across the frozen tundra by radio telegraph. Doctors in Seattle, Washington, signaled back that they had serum that could be immediately flown to Nome. But the weather in Alaska was too frigid and stormy for those long-ago planes. Ships couldn't make it through either as the waterways were frozen over.

Dog-Team Special Delivery

Then Anchorage, Alaska, answered the frantic call. They had serum that could be shipped by train to Nenana, in the center of the state. But how could it be transported the additional 1,085 kilometers (674 miles) to Nome, on Alaska's coast? Officials decided the only way was by a relay of dogsled teams.

The trip usually took a dog team a month. But children were dying. How much faster could the series of dog teams run?

On January 27, the diphtheria serum finally arrived by train in Nenana. The relay west to the endangered city began.

WOOF!

The diphtheria serum was wrapped in fur. It froze several times during its icy journey but was still effective.

Northern DOGS

The best-known northern dogs are huskies (Siberian and Alaskan), Samoyeds, and malamutes. Huskies are fast and energetic. Their eyes are typically pale blue and their coats are gray, black, reddish, or white.

Malamutes' coats are similar to huskies' in color, but their eyes are usually brown. As well, these dogs are larger than huskies. Malamutes are smart and confident dogs. Although they're slow, they can move heavy loads.

Did you know the correct way to pronounce Samoyed is "SAM-ee-ed"? These fluffy white dogs with dark eyes were bred to help with herding as well as to pull sleds. They're very friendly and make good watchdogs.

The Relay Begins

The first team of dogs and a musher (the person who drives a dog team and sled) set out in freezing weather with the serum lashed to the sled behind them. The temperature kept dropping—sometimes to as low as minus 53°C (minus 64°F). The precious cargo was transferred from one sled to the next when each dog team completed its portion of the relay. Each section was about 52 kilometers (32 miles) long. On January 30, two dogs nearly froze, so the musher harnessed himself to the sled to help the dogs pull it.

The next day, near the town of Shaktoolik, the serum was passed to musher Leonhard Seppala and his lead dog Togo, the fastest dog in the state. The team had just run 274 kilometers from Nome (170 miles) to join the relay. But as soon as Leonhard had the serum, Togo and the team took off again.

Malamute

Samoyed

Husky

Leonhard Seppala with his team of hard-working dogs that earned the records for carrying the diphtheria serum the longest and the fastest. Togo is on the far left.

Not Sled-Dog Material?

Togo hadn't always been such a top dog. For one thing, he didn't look like a typical sled dog. He was small and his black, brown, and gray coat always looked a little dirty. As a puppy back in 1914, Togo continually got in the way of the working sled dogs, trying to get them to play. So Leonhard had put the little Siberian husky into a harness to try to control him. To the musher's amazement, Togo immediately settled down.

As the team ran that day, Leonhard kept stopping the dogs and moving Togo up the line. By the end of the day, Togo was sharing the lead, even though he was just a puppy. On his first day in harness, this wonder dog had run 120 kilometers (75 miles), an impressive distance for an inexperienced dog.

WOOF!

Huskies look almost the same as Arctic wolves, but huskies carry their tails high and curled over their backs. Wolves' tails always hang down.

Built FOR Survival

A dog is a predator and its body has evolved to make it an effective hunter. Since dogs are carnivores (meat eaters), their teeth are designed for catching, holding, and tearing meat.

Chasing prey—or, in the case of most pets, toys—requires fast action, and dogs' bodies are running machines. They walk on their toes, which lengthens their legs and increases their stride. Their fused wrist bones make their feet stronger.

The bottom of a dog's paw is covered by thick pads that protect the paw and give it a good grip on many surfaces, including ice. The nails also give a dog traction when it runs.

Dogs are better at staying warm than keeping cool. They only produce sweat on areas not covered with fur, such as the nose and paw pads. To lose heat, dogs pant and hang their tongues out. Shallow, quick breaths help evaporate the moisture on the tongue and that cools the tongue.

A dog's tail may be straight, curled, or corkscrew; bushy or thin. The main way dogs use their tails is to communicate to each other, which helps them get along in a pack.

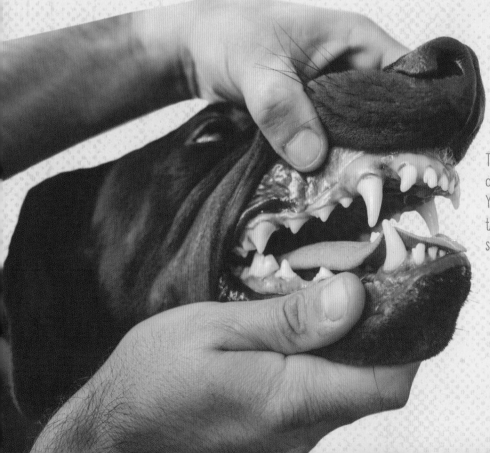

Those long pointed teeth are called canine teeth. You've got four of them too. They hold food firmly so it can be torn apart.

Dogs have pulled sleds for Inuit people for thousands of years. When sled-dog pups are six months old, they begin pulling small logs to get a feel for it.

Dangerous Decision

Togo became one of the best lead sled dogs, with an amazing ability to sense danger. With his team racing along behind him toward Nome, Togo reached the shore of Norton Sound, an inlet of the Bering Sea on Alaska's coast. At that moment, Leonhard halted the dogs.

The musher had a tough decision to make: Should they risk taking a shortcut across the frozen, treacherous sound or go all the way around it? Going around would take a lot longer, but the powerful winds on the sound threatened to break up the ice at any second.

Leonhard decided to let Togo make the choice. The musher held his breath as the leader stepped out onto the sound. The brave dog led the team swiftly across the jagged ice, their paws slipping on the slick surface. But Togo steadily guided the sled to the land on the other side. Leonhard found out later that just a few hours after this perilous crossing, the ice broke up.

Teamwork

There are four types of dogs in a team. At the front are the leaders, the dogs that follow the musher's commands and set the pace. Today, there are usually two lead dogs, but at the time of the serum run, there was often only one.

Next are the two swing dogs. They help turn the team in the direction the lead dogs are guiding.

The pair of team dogs comes next. They power the sled and help maintain the speed.

At the back, just in front of the sled, are the two wheel dogs. They pull and steer the sled, for instance, going wide on a turn to guide the sled around trees.

"Scrub Dog"

Togo's team carried the antitoxin serum 146 kilometers (91 miles) to the next musher, who then passed it on to Gunnar Kaasen, one of Alaska's most experienced mushers. Gunnar's lead dog was named Balto.

Like Togo, Balto was a Siberian husky. No one had originally expected much from him either. He was considered slow, only good for carrying heavy loads, not for racing. Balto was called a scrub dog, meaning second-rate.

But Balto was smart and strong. Gunnar believed Balto had good instincts and could lead the team through the blizzards. It was the black-and-white dog's first time in lead position.

Chill OUT

Northern dogs have adapted to survive extreme cold. Most important is their double-layered coat. The outer layer is coarse and straight and keeps the undercoat clean. That undercoat is dense and soft and keeps the dog insulated. The plumy tail covers the dog's nose while it sleeps and traps the dog's warm breath around its face.

Their blood-circulation system has evolved to protect their feet. If their paws were the same temperature as the rest of their body, they would melt the snow around them and the water would freeze, chilling their paws. So these dogs' circulation system feeds cool blood to their feet and warms the blood before it goes back to their heart.

Dogs curl up when they sleep, to keep warm and to protect their stomach and vital organs.

Balto Saves the Team

Gunnar and the team were almost across the frozen Topkok River when Balto suddenly stopped. Gunnar battled the winds to make his way to Balto's side, where he saw open water, deep enough to have soaked Balto's feet.

The frigid water would have frozen all the dogs' legs, making them unable to run and possibly causing permanent damage, if not for Balto's sharp instincts. Gunnar dried the dog's feet and soon the team was running again, along a different route.

Gunnar Kaasen was very proud of Balto and his team of sled dogs. They ran almost their entire leg of the relay in the dark. Balto was named after Samuel Balto, an explorer from northern Scandinavia.

A Long Way from Nome

Balto led the team to the next shelter, where a fresh team of dogs would take over. But no one had expected Balto's dogs to make it through the wind storm, so the driver and dogs were asleep.

Gunnar knew it would take precious time to wake the next musher and get his team ready. Balto and his team didn't seem tired and were still keeping up a good pace. Gunnar decided to keep going.

On they sped, through the cold, dark night. Then—disaster! A vicious gust of wind sent the sled and the dogs soaring into the air. The minute they hit the ground, luckily with none of the dogs hurt, Gunnar began untangling the dogs' lines. But he soon realized with horror that the serum had disappeared.

Gunnar scrabbled in the snow with his bare hands until finally he felt something in the heavy snowdrifts. Gunnar breathed a sigh of relief as his icy fingers closed around the package. He fastened it to the sled, and the team took off again.

Nome at Last

It wasn't yet daybreak on February 2, 1925, when Balto led his tired, nearly frozen team into Nome. The city was saved. The 20 mushers and more than 100 fearless dogs had done the near impossible and carried the serum to Nome in just 127.5 hours, or less than six days.

Forgotten Heroes

Because Balto and his team had run the final 90-kilometer (56-mile) lap and actually brought the serum to Nome, they became more famous than any of the other dogs. People all over North America wanted to see the courageous dogs that had saved a city.

But by 1927, most people had forgotten about Balto. He and the six other dogs from his team ended up in a carnival-style museum of oddities and curiosities in Los Angeles. George Kimble, a businessman from Cleveland, Ohio, visited them there and was outraged to see the heroic dogs chained in a dark, stuffy room.

George agreed to buy the dogs from the museum owner so he could give them a good home in Cleveland. But the dogs cost $2,000—that's almost $27,000 today—and he had just two weeks to raise the money.

WOOF!

A "three-dog night" means it's so cold you need three dogs in bed with you to keep warm. The phrase may be from the Arctic or from Australia, where the desert can be very cold at night.

WORLD-FAMOUS SLED-DOG Race

The 1925 serum run to Nome is remembered with the Iditarod Trail Sled Dog Race. Each year, in early March, more than 50 mushers—mostly from Alaska—and about 1,000 dogs race from Anchorage to Nome, approximately 1,688 kilometers (1,049 miles). That's like the distance from New York City to Orlando, Florida! The fastest time is about 8 days and 13 hours, a record set in 2014.

The trail gets its name from the town of Iditarod, an Athabascan village. In the early 1900s, it was in the midst of rich goldfields, but today, it is a ghost town. The Iditarod Trail was first used by Inupiaq and Athabascan Native people and later the gold miners.

The Race Is On—Again!

Across America, radio stations and newspapers carried pleas for donations to the Balto Fund. Schoolkids, office staff, factory workers, stores, and restaurants gathered funds. In 10 days, the full amount was raised. Balto and his team were saved.

On March 19, 1927, the dogs arrived in Cleveland as crowds cheered. They were taken to Brookside Zoo (now Cleveland Metroparks Zoo), where the dogs were finally well cared for.

The End of the Trail

Balto was 14 years old when he died in March 1933. His body was preserved by a taxidermist, and you can still see it at the Cleveland Museum of Natural History.

Although Togo and his team ran the longest and most dangerous part of the route, he never received the same fame as Balto. But Togo was loved by people in Alaska. When he died in 1929, he was preserved, like Balto. Today, you can see Togo at the Iditarod Trail Sled Dog Race Headquarters museum in Wasilla, Alaska.

This life-size statue of Balto stands in Central Park in New York City. Some parts are shiny thanks to all the children and adults who touch the statue.

CHAPTER 5
A REAL Buddy:
America's First GUIDE DOG 1928

MORRIS FRANK LISTENED TO HIS FATHER EXCITEDLY. The 19-year-old, who had been partially blind since he was 6, had become totally blind due to a boxing accident when he was 16. What his dad was reading to him seemed incredible. The article, published in the *Saturday Evening Post* magazine on November 5, 1927, was written by an American named Dorothy Harrison Eustis, who was living in Switzerland. She described a program she'd visited in Germany where dogs were trained as guides for soldiers blinded in World War I (see page 26).

When Morris was young, many blind people led difficult lives as beggars.

What bothered Morris most about his blindness was having no independence. He couldn't go where he wanted, when he wanted. If Morris wanted to get his hair cut, his dad dropped him off at the barbershop in downtown Nashville, Tennessee, on his way to work. Then Morris was stuck there until his dad picked him up on his lunch hour.

Morris couldn't stop thinking about the article. He decided to write to Dorothy and ask if she knew where he could get a guide dog.

"I Want One of Those Dogs!"

"Is what you say really true?" Morris wrote to Dorothy. "If so, I want one of those dogs! And I am not alone. Thousands of blind like me abhor being dependent on others." To convince her to assist him, he continued, "Help me and I will help them. Train me and I will bring back my dog and show people here how a blind man can be absolutely on his own. We can then set up an instruction center in this country to give all those here who want it a chance at a new life."

In those days, most people who were blind couldn't get jobs. They had to rely on other people. Morris's father was well off, so Morris could hire someone to assist him. But one of Morris's guides sometimes became bored and left him to find his own way home! Morris thought if he had a guide dog, that wouldn't happen again.

WOOF!

National Guide Dog Month is September, when guide dogs are celebrated and money is raised for guide-dog schools.

GERMANY

FRANCE
Vevey●
SWITZERLAND

UNITED STATES
●New York
●Nashville

Atlantic Ocean

The Package Has Been Shipped

Weeks passed while Morris waited to hear from Dorothy. She had been training dogs to work with the army and the police. But Morris's letter made her want to help blind people too. So on February 9, 1928, she telephoned him. Morris must have been surprised since phone calls between Europe and the United States were unusual then. Dorothy asked him if he was willing to travel to Switzerland to be matched with a guide dog. "Mrs. Eustis," Morris replied, "to get my independence back, I'd go to hell."

Morris set out on his journey in April 1928. He was traveling alone, and since he couldn't look after himself, he was classified as a package! When the ship arrived in France, Morris was put in a shed full of baggage, just like all the other packages. There he stood until someone took him to the train station. Morris couldn't wait to be paired with a guide dog so he could live like other people.

Dogs GO TO WORK

Hearing dogs, also called signal dogs, help people who are deaf or hard of hearing. These dogs alert owners to ringing phones, street-crossing signals, and even buzzing smoke alarms.

Mobility-assistance dogs help their owners balance on stairs or stand up. Medical-response dogs bring their owners medications or, in the case of an owner with diabetes, alert the person that her blood sugar is too low or high.

Sniffer-seizure dogs help people who have epilepsy or severe allergies. When their owners have seizures, the dogs get them to safety or bring medication.

Psychiatric-service dogs can help people with post-traumatic stress disorder (PTSD) or who suffer from depression or other mental health issues.

Cool-Headed CANINES

Two guide dogs showed great courage on September 11, 2001, when terrorists attacked the World Trade Center in New York City (see page 82). Salty and his owner, Omar Rivera, were on the seventy-first floor when the plane hit the north tower. Salty refused to leave Omar and led him downstairs and out of the tower.

Roselle calmly led her owner, Michael Hingson, through the smoke and confusion. She guided Michael and 30 other people down almost 1,500 steps to safety.

Salty and Roselle were honored with a joint Dickin Medal. Roselle was named a 2011 American Hero Dog.

Roselle, left, and Salty, middle, receiving their Dickin Medals. Appollo, right, accepted an award for all search and rescue dogs that worked at the World Trade Center and Pentagon.

Morris Gets a Kiss

Dorothy met Morris when he arrived in Vevey, Switzerland, and immediately noticed how hesitantly he moved. She hoped a guide dog would change that. The next day, Dorothy introduced Morris to a beautiful, smart, well-trained German shepherd.

There was just one problem. The dog Dorothy wanted Morris to work with was named Kiss. Morris imagined how people would make fun of him when he called his dog by a name like that. Morris renamed the dog Buddy (though she was a female).

WOOF!

You can see a video of Morris and Buddy online to hear in Morris's own words how important Buddy was. Search for "Seeing Eye Morris Frank Buddy YouTube."

Buddy Trains Her Human

Now the hard work began. Morris would have to learn to follow Buddy. First, Morris was taught to put a stiff harness on her, one that would let him feel her movements. Since he couldn't see what he was doing, he accidentally poked her in the eye and pinched her ear with the strap, but Buddy stood quietly.

Finally, the day came for Buddy to guide Morris. They set off together across an open lawn. "The harness came alive in my hands," Morris said later. "After years of fumbling with a cane at a slow pace, I felt like I was floating across the yard with Buddy."

Morris still had lots to learn. He had to be sure to keep the harness in his left hand and his right arm close to his body so he wouldn't bump into things. Sometimes Morris missed the signals Buddy was giving him and walked into closed doors and other obstacles. He had to pay attention if Buddy hesitated and learn to trust his dog.

Morris said, "Buddy delivered to me the divine gift of freedom." He also said, "I could feel every movement of her shoulders as she walked," thanks to her harness.

Dog DATA

Train THAT DOG

Dogs can be trained to do so many tasks to help people because they're pack animals. That means they're used to obeying a leader, or "alpha male" (which, of course, can also be a woman, when it comes to a human dog leader). They love to have the attention. So dogs will learn tricks and tasks to please their owners and achieve the goal of being noticed.

Dogs that are bred for herding or hunting are faster at picking up cues and so are usually easier to train. These breeds include border collies, German shepherds, and golden retrievers. A dog that has a mind of its own, such as a basset hound, beagle, and bulldog, is tougher to train. These dogs aren't stupid—they just have different, more independent personalities.

Although all dogs learn differently, it's much easier for them to learn spoken commands if they're given at the same time as hand signals or gestures. Training a dog well also depends a lot on the trainer's patience. Young adult dogs, from about two to five years old, learn more easily than puppies (up to nine months) or "teenage" dogs (nine to fourteen months).

Puppies chew shoes because they're teething or bored. It can be hard to train them to stop.

It's amazing the tricks a dog can be trained to perform!

Buddy Takes Charge

Buddy had been taught to pull back and stand at curbs to give Morris time to find the edge with his foot. At stairs, Buddy had been trained to sit down to alert Morris to them. Buddy had to figure out how much space Morris required and where he could move safely. She learned to ignore other dogs and distractions like squirrels.

Buddy also learned "intelligent disobedience." That meant that if Morris told her to go forward, but Buddy could see there was a low-hanging branch or other danger, she would take Morris in another direction.

One day, as Buddy and Morris walked into a nearby Swiss town, Buddy suddenly veered off the road, yanking Morris up a steep hill. He couldn't understand why his dog was acting so oddly until he heard the clattering of hooves.

A team of horses was rushing down the road out of control. Morris could have been killed, but Buddy had sensed the danger and immediately pulled him aside. What a dog!

Buddy saved Morris from the runaway horses because she was trained to think for herself and take care of her owner. Morris quickly learned to follow Buddy, give her complete attention, and let her be the leader.

WOOF!

The average pet dog can understand words and language at about the same level as a two-year-old human.

Buddy Meets the Challenge

After a couple of months, it was time for Morris to head home, back across the ocean. But this time, he could go wherever he wanted on the ship, thanks to Buddy.

The pair arrived in New York City on June 11, 1928. Immediately, Morris began trying to get publicity for Dorothy's guide-dog program. Reporters challenged him to cross West Street, a road so busy and dangerous it was known as Death Street. To the journalists' amazement, Buddy safely guided Morris through the roaring traffic.

The reporters rushed to their newsrooms to write articles about the talented dog. Morris sent a telegram to Dorothy to let her know how things were going. It had just one word: Success.

Buddy's head moved from side to side as she watched the traffic and safely led Morris across the street.

IS THAT DOG... *Reading?*

It's hard to believe, but there's even a type of service dog that helps children learn to read. Kids are paired with dogs, sometimes ones from animal shelters, and the children read aloud to their furry friends. The kids gain confidence in their reading because the dogs don't complain or criticize if the children read slowly or make mistakes.

The dogs are happy to have someone paying attention to them and are attentive listeners. The children learn or improve a skill without any stress. It's a win-win situation.

SuperDogs!

Dogs can be trained to do many things besides being service dogs. Some learn to perform fantastic tricks. The SuperDogs are a group of amazing pooches that tour North America performing at fairs, exhibitions, and special events. They catch Frisbees, jump over obstacles, soar through hoops, and even dance. During their shows, music blares and lights flash, but these dogs stay focused.

The SuperDogs come in many shapes, sizes, and breeds. About one-third of them are rescue dogs, which means they were adopted from animal shelters. But they all have lots of energy, love to play, and learn in no time at all.

The SuperDogs learn amazing tricks through patient training and the dogs' intense desire to please their trainers.

Buddy Changes the Law

When he first began traveling on trains with Buddy, Morris was often told she couldn't sit in the passenger compartment with him. So he met with President Herbert Hoover in 1930 and asked for laws giving blind people the right to go with their dogs wherever sighted people could go. Buddy was so smart and well behaved that she impressed politicians and lawmakers, which helped get the laws passed.

By 1935, all trains in the United States allowed guide dogs to stay with their owners. By 1956, every American state had passed laws that guaranteed blind people with guide dogs the right to have access to public places. The Americans with Disabilities Act was passed in 1990. It stated that no one with special needs could be discriminated against.

Today, National Seeing Eye Dog Day is celebrated on January 29, the day Morris opened America's first guide-dog training school. Buddy was the first formally trained guide dog in the United States. Plays and movies were produced about her and Morris.

Buddy died in 1938, and Morris went on to have many more guide dogs. He named them all Buddy, in honor of the smart, faithful friend who gave him his freedom.

Morris worked to "to get Buddy accepted all over America with no more fuss than if she were a cane."

Morris fought to have guide dogs accepted everywhere.

No dogs
Except guide dogs

CHAPTER 6

MILITARY Guard Dogs:

WORLD WAR II'S DOGS FOR DEFENSE

1939-1945

THERE WAS NO MOON as the intruder quietly crept over the sand toward the lone sentry. The wind blew coldly off the Atlantic Ocean, and the man hoped it would carry his scent away from the dog standing on duty with his handler.

In December 1941, Pearl Harbor was attacked by 353 Japanese planes, killing more than 2,400 Americans.

Closer and closer the dark figure inched, until he was hiding behind a nearby sand dune. A little farther and he would be past the sentry.

Suddenly, roaring out of the night came the guard dog, galloping straight to the spot where the man crouched. This had actually just been a test of the sentry and his dog. While the sentry didn't do so well, the dog passed with flying colors. No wonder the American army depended on its well-trained dogs for protection during World War II.

The Country Goes to War

On December 7, 1941, Americans were shocked to hear news reports that Japanese bombers had attacked the United States naval base in Pearl Harbor, Hawaii. So far, the United States had stayed out of World War II, but the next day, American president Franklin D. Roosevelt declared war on Japan, and the United States entered the war.

WOOF!

In April 2016, German shepherd Lucca became the first United States Marine Corps dog awarded the Dickin Medal. She sniffed out bombs in Afghanistan and saved many lives.

THE GUARD DOG THAT Saved a City

One dark night in 456 BCE, Persian soldiers decided to attack the city of Corinth, Greece. They knew the soldiers of the town were fast asleep in the nearby citadel.

But as the Persians snuck into Corinth, they were attacked by the 50 guard dogs trained to protect the city. The dogs fought bravely, but all of them—except one—were killed.

Soter (which means "savior" in Greek) ran to the citadel and awoke the sleeping soldiers in time for them to fight off the invaders and save the town. For his bravery, Soter earned an engraved silver collar.

Dogs for Defense

In January 1942, the Dogs for Defense program was set up. The aim was to provide dogs for sentry duty to guard against attacks on the coast of the United States and on its harbors and ports. Radio announcements and newspaper articles (people didn't have televisions in their homes yet) urged patriotic dog owners to donate their pets to help win the war. Loyal Americans sent in close to 19,000!

An eight-year-old boy from California offered his dog: "I have a large Australian shepherd dog about two-and-one-half years old, that is a very good hunter ... He sure likes to kill skunks." Actress Mary Pickford, known as "America's Sweetheart," donated her German shepherd.

At first the army classified 32 breeds as war dogs. By 1944, the list was reduced to just 7 that tended to be the easiest to train: Belgian sheepdogs, collies, Doberman pinschers (right), Eskimo dogs, German shepherds, malamutes, and Siberian huskies. Dogs that weren't accepted for the program were sent back to their owners. Successful dogs became part of the war dog program, newly named the K-9 Corps.

GERMANY

AFGHANISTAN

JAPAN

Pacific
Ocean

UNITED
STATES

VIRGINIA

IRAQ

PAKISTAN

Atlantic
Ocean

Pearl Harbor

HAWAII

VIETNAM

GUAM

Training Begins

The first training center for the K-9 Corps was set up in August 1942 in Virginia. It could hold more than 1,800 dogs, but a few months later, more training centers had to be opened.

Most dogs were trained for sentry duty. These dogs patrolled the coastline, watching for enemies landing, and guarded factories and plants producing weapons and vehicle parts for soldiers and the war effort.

The dogs trained for eight to twelve weeks. Basic training included learning spoken commands and hand signals, learning to stay silent, and remaining calm when bombs exploded or guns were fired.

Dogs more than five years old were found to be too set in their ways for the specialized training. K-9 Corps members also had to be a neutral color such as black, gray, or brown—white or beige dogs were too conspicuous.

K-9s were trained to detect an intruder by his scent. Rather than bark and scare away the trespasser, dogs silently led their handler to the invader. The dogs even learned to crawl on their bellies so the grasses along the shoreline would conceal them.

Dogs that helped Marines in World War II were often Dobermans and were nicknamed "Devil Dogs."

ALL Shapes & Sizes

There are more than 700 dog breeds, from the Chihuahua, weighing about 2.3 kilograms (5 pounds) and 20 centimeters (8 inches) tall, to the Irish wolfhound, about 63.5 kilograms (140 pounds) and 86 centimeters (34 inches) tall. Most fit into one of five groups: companion dogs, guard dogs, herding dogs, hunting dogs, and working dogs.

Dogs exist in such variety because people living in different places and climates have crossbred them for a wide range of tasks. Most breeds are a few hundred years old.

Chihuahua

Irish wolfhound

Poodle

Did you know the French poodle originated in Germany? The name comes from the German word for puddle. Historians say the pompoms of hair in the common way of grooming poodles were to keep their joints warm when hunters shaved the rest of the dogs' body to help them swim faster.

All dogs have 321 bones and 42 permanent teeth. But some breeds have strange features: the chow has a purple tongue, while the Norwegian lundehund has six toes on each foot—most dogs have only four.

Norwegian lundehund

K-9 Corps to the Rescue

During the war, Japanese submarines were spotted lurking off America's Pacific Coast and German U-boats (submarines) were observed patrolling the Atlantic Coast. But no foreign soldiers or spies landed, perhaps because they were terrified of facing a howling, snapping dog.

The K-9 Corps kept people safe in other ways too. One cold night, a coastguardsman became furious when his dog wouldn't obey his command to walk forward. When he shone his flashlight past the dog, the patroller realized he was on the edge of a cliff. The dog had saved his life!

On another cold night, a patrolman fainted on duty. Nora, a coast guard German shepherd, found the man. She couldn't rouse him, so she grabbed his cap in her teeth and raced to the closest coast guard station. After alerting the men there, she galloped off and found another patrolman guarding the area. Nora led him to the unconscious coastguardsman just in time—he was close to death because of the frigid weather.

WOOF!

The top three most popular breeds in North America are, first, Labrador retriever; second, German shepherd; and third, golden retriever.

Nora received a medal for saving the life of Coast Guardsman Evans E. Mitchell, shown with her.

Cerberus & Fluffy

The dog that guards the entrance to hell is a little unusual—it has three heads! According to Greek mythology, Cerberus (below), the "Hellhound of Hades," prevents souls from leaving the underworld.

Another famous, but thankfully not real, dog with three heads is Fluffy, from the Harry Potter books. He is owned by Harry's friend Rubeus Hagrid, and is very loyal to Hagrid.

Both Cerberus and Fluffy are huge guard dogs, but they have one weakness. They can be put to sleep with music, which is how Harry and his friends managed to sneak by Fluffy in one of their adventures.

During World War I, dogs pulled volley guns, large guns similar to cannons.

Messengers, Scouts, and Trackers

Some military dogs were also trained to lay down wire (to help with communications and explosives), deliver messages, search for wounded soldiers, scout, attack, and track. They were also good at pulling supply cars and machine guns over rough ground. The dogs could trot through dense underbrush that was too thick for horses or mules to push through.

The dogs were so smart they could be trained to realize that if all the members of their gun crew were killed in action, they should head back to base, pulling the guns with them. That not only saved the dogs' lives but also made sure the guns weren't captured by the enemy.

On the Battlefield

In 1944, seven platoons with war dogs arrived in Europe, while eight platoons, also with dogs, were sent to the islands in the Pacific, where the United States was also at war. Most of these dogs had been trained as scouts to detect enemy soldiers. When the platoon arrived in Guam, in the northwestern Pacific Ocean, the soldiers there laughed at the dogs. What could animals do to help?

The soldiers weren't laughing for long. They soon saw how the dogs kept them safe. The K-9 Corps members could hear stealth attacks long before the humans, as well as sniff out ambushes. It wasn't long before any soldier heading off to scout out an area always made sure he took a dog along.

WOOF!

Piper is a guard dog at an airport in Traverse City, Michigan. The border collie scares birds away from the runways as planes take off and land. Look for Piper on Instagram.

While serving on the front lines in Guam in 1944, Peppy went missing for three days. When she returned, the American soldiers quickly had her wounds bandaged.

The K-9 Corps Heads Home

By 1945, when the war ended, the army, navy, and coast guard had trained more than 10,400 dogs. Almost 9,300 served their country on sentry duty. Nearly 3,650 dogs were used by the coast guard for beach patrols.

After the war, many dogs were "de-trained"—including being taught that people are friendly and how not to react to loud noises—and were returned to their original owners or put up for adoption. Some went to work for police departments and security companies or became guide dogs for blind people.

THE Wonder FROM DOWN UNDER

During World War II, many air crew in Darwin, Australia, owed their lives to a dog named Gunner. One day in 1942, the fliers noticed Gunner whining and jumping up anxiously. A few minutes later, Japanese planes attacked.

Gunner was a kelpie, an Australian sheepdog known for its acute hearing. Again and again, he alerted the soldiers to incoming air attacks so the men could seek shelter. Sometimes Gunner barked his warning 20 minutes before the planes arrived, long before they appeared on radar.

Gunner never reacted when Allied aircraft flew over. But he always knew when enemy planes were approaching.

Gunner broke his leg the first time Darwin was raided by enemy aircraft, so he was always on the alert for attacks.

Better Than Machines

After the dogs in the K-9 Corps were returned to their owners, the army replaced the volunteered dogs with ones that were purchased.

About 1,500 dogs performed sentry duty during the Korean War (1950–1953). In the Vietnam War, which was fought between 1954 and 1975, dogs patrolled compounds to protect American soldiers. About 4,000 dogs guarded airplane bases and other army buildings in Vietnam.

Military dogs have served in Iraq and Afghanistan as guards and to sniff out bombs. Some dogs can identify the smell of explosives (scientists call this a "vapor wake") on suicide bombers as they push through crowded streets. The dogs then lead soldiers to the suspected bomber. Despite advances in technology, Military Working Dogs (MWDs) still detect bombs more accurately and more quickly than state-of-the-art machines.

The incredible dogs in the K-9 Corps can slide down ropes, and some can run as fast as 64 kilometers per hour (40 miles per hour).

WOOf!

The basenji is the only breed of dog that can't bark. It has an unusually shaped larynx (voice box), so it makes a yodel sound instead.

This dog is patrolling in Afghanistan after an improvised explosive device (IED) explosion.

PARADOGS!

Sometimes when the army wants to get military dogs to a site quickly, the dogs are parachuted in with their trainers. Smaller dogs can be strapped, facing forward, to the soldiers' chests. Larger dogs are placed in slings and hang across the soldiers' bodies, at about waist height.

Dogs may wear Doggles to protect their eyes as they drop through the air. They may also wear muzzles to keep their mouths from being injured when they land.

Paradogs were first used in World War II to locate land mines, keep watch, and warn against enemies. They still accompany U.S. Navy SEALs when the soldiers have to be dropped into action.

In May 2011, a group of Navy SEALs in Pakistan were hot on the trail of terrorist Osama bin Laden, who had planned the attacks on New York City's World Trade Center on September 11, 2001 (see page 82).

A vital team member was a Belgian Malinois named Cairo. He was there to alert the SEALs to any Pakistani security forces, help search for any hidden doors or rooms in the compound where bin Laden was believed to be hiding, and track anyone who tried to get away. Cairo was the first of the team to hear and smell the al-Qaeda leader and made sure he didn't escape.

Today, breeds used to guard American military bases include Labrador retrievers and Malinois, as well as German shepherds. Some of them wear vests as protection from knives or bullets. High-tech equipment, such as an infrared camera or a Global Positioning System (GPS) device, can be attached to the vest. In desert areas, the dogs may also wear "Doggles," special goggles to protect their eyes from blowing sand.

CHAPTER 7

Sniffer Dog

SAVES THE DAY:

AIRPLANE EXPLOSION

prevented

1972

"GOOD MORNING, TRANS WORLD AIRLINES.
How may I help you?"

But this caller on March 7, 1972, wasn't phoning to find out about flight times or to buy a plane ticket. Instead, he informed the terrified Trans World Airlines (TWA) staffer that he had placed bombs on four of the airline's planes flying that day.

The caller then demanded $2 million or he would blow up a plane every six hours. Before he hung up, he shocked the TWA receptionist even more by announcing the first bomb was scheduled to detonate at 1:00 p.m., just a few hours away.

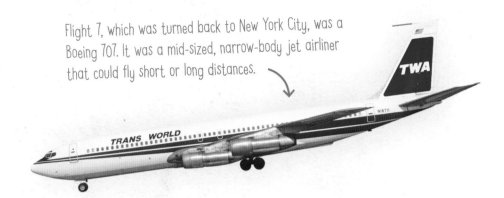

Flight 7, which was turned back to New York City, was a Boeing 707. It was a mid-sized, narrow-body jet airliner that could fly short or long distances.

Emergency Landing

While some TWA staff began to pack the cash into duffel bags as demanded, emergency workers jumped into action. All planes were grounded since there was no way of knowing which ones were in danger. They had to be searched rapidly and carefully to make sure they were safe.

But Flight 7 had already been in the air for 15 minutes. If it blew up high in the skies, there would be devastating damage. It had to be brought down to earth and fast. The captain was surprised to receive an emergency call telling him to turn back to New York's John F. Kennedy International Airport and land as quickly as possible.

WOOF!

A bloodhound can trace scents more than 300 hours old. It's such a good sniffer breed because its big, floppy ears fan smells to its nose.

CANADA

UNITED STATES

New York

Atlantic Ocean

Today, you can often see dogs in airports inspecting passengers' baggage. This dog is checking to make sure travelers aren't carrying liquids, such as drinks or lotions, onto airplanes in their carry-on luggage.

Detective Brandy Is on the Case

The Boeing 707 streaked back to New York, touching down at 12:10 p.m. The moment the pilot landed, the 45 passengers and 7 crew members were rushed off the plane. Then the pilot speedily taxied the aircraft to the distant end of the runway, as far as possible from the terminal.

Expert staff searched the plane and found no trace of a bomb, but they still weren't satisfied. Luckily, the New York Police Department had a secret weapon: a German shepherd named Brandy. She was one of the first dogs trained to find bombs. By chance, she happened to be at the airport that day because she was giving a demonstration on bomb-sniffing. There was no national sniffer-dog program yet—Brandy had been trained in a university lab.

SNIFFING IN THE WILD

When scientists are trying to find out how many wild animals live in an area, they sometimes call on dogs for help. But these are specially trained pooches, taught to sniff out the animals' droppings, known as scat. From owls to bears to salamanders, scat-detection dogs can do the job.

Why use dogs? One reason is that they can cover larger areas in less time than humans can. They're willing to climb mountains or clamber over rocks to track down the scat. Once the dogs lead the scientists to it, they can study the scat to find out what the animals are eating, their sex, and their state of health.

Hidden in Plain Sight

Brandy and her handler raced out to the plane. The canine detective climbed on board and began checking for explosives. She trotted along the aisle, sniffing to the left and right. When she sat down by a black briefcase to indicate that she smelled explosives in it, the expert searchers were disappointed and frustrated.

The bomb squad was sure Brandy was wrong. After all, the case was marked CREW and briefcases like this were found on all flight decks since they contained flight manuals. The pilot had seen the case earlier and ignored it.

Brandy wouldn't budge, so the explosives expert carefully opened the briefcase. There were no manuals inside—it contained 2.3 kilograms (5 pounds) of C-4, an explosive that looks and feels like modeling clay. But this was no art supply! There was enough C-4 in the briefcase to destroy the whole plane.

WOOF!

In 1966, the collie Pickles sniffed out the location of the stolen World Cup soccer trophy. His collar is on display in the National Football Museum in Manchester, England.

This bomb squad detective was very proud of Brandy's work when she found the explosives-filled briefcase.

Countdown

The timer attached to the explosive showed there were only minutes left before the bomb would explode. Precious seconds ticked by as the explosives expert worked on dismantling the device. If the anonymous caller had been telling the truth, the bomb was timed to blow up at 1:00 p.m.

In the nick of time, with just 12 minutes left, the expert managed to disarm the bomb. Everyone was safe and the plane was in one piece. Brandy had saved the day.

woOf!

Two United States Customs and Border Protection dogs were so good at sniffing out drugs on the American/ Mexican border that Mexican drug lords put a $300,000 bounty on their heads.

A Dog's Nose Knows

A dog is much better than a human at detecting odors. Its nose has 20 to 40 times more odor receptors, the sites where scent molecules are detected. While a human has about 5 million odor receptors, a bloodhound has 300 million! The part of a dog's brain that analyzes smells is 40 times bigger than the same area in a human's brain.

A dog has other advantages over a human when it comes to sniffing. It's better at pulling in a big sample of a scent since its nose is longer and bigger. Also, a dog is closer to the ground so it can get its nose closer to most smells. Some scientists have said most dogs are 1,000 times better at smelling than a human. Others say some dogs are one million times better!

A dog's nose has a bony shelf inside that human noses don't have. Odor molecules stick here and build up. This makes scents stronger, which helps dogs smell even faint odors.

Dog DATA

Dog's Senses

Besides their amazing sense of smell, dogs can hear about four times better than people can. That's because a dog's ear canal (the narrow tube where sound enters the ear) is four times longer than a human's. The extra length makes a better funnel to move sound to the eardrum.

Dogs don't see color as well as people can, but they're not totally color-blind. They see movement and light much better than humans do and have better night vision. However, they can't see fine details as well as we can.

People have about six times as many taste buds as dogs do, so a dog's sense of taste isn't great. That could explain some of the disgusting junk they eat! They get more information from smelling than tasting. A dog also has an organ at the top of its mouth that lets it "taste" some smells.

Dogs may even have an extra sense—scientists at universities in Germany and the Czech Republic have shown that dogs align their bodies with the earth's magnetic field when they poop. Now the scientists have to figure out why!

How to Train a Sniffer Dog

Training a sniffer (or detection) dog like Brandy involves repetition, games, and play, as well as praise and treats for the dog. The trainer begins by teaching the dog to play fetch or tug-of-war. This part of the training is easy because most dogs love playing these games. As the dog plays with its favorite toy, it is taught commands such as "Search" or "Find."

Next, the toy is covered with the smell of the substance that the dog will be expected to sniff out. As the dog gets better and better at tracking down its scented toy, the toy is removed so the dog is simply searching for the smell. It takes most dogs two to four months to learn the basics of sniffing for bombs.

A soldier hoists a tactical explosive detection dog as they train for rescue missions.

A soldier will carry his dog to help build loyalty, teamwork, and trust between the pair.

Striker has been trained to detect brown tree snakes.

Scent Detection

Dogs are taught either passive or aggressive scent detection. With passive detection, the dog is trained to just sit when it smells the target scent, as Brandy did. In aggressive detection, the dog will paw or bark at the object.

A sniffer dog can pick out particular smells, even when there are many others around. How does the canine detective do it? When the dog takes a sniff, that action actually reshapes its nose so the smells it breathes in are channeled directly to the dog's odor receptors.

The signal then moves from the nose to the part of the brain that processes smells. There the scent is interpreted, and if it's the odor the dog is trained to search for, it will indicate to its handler that it has tracked down the object.

When Brandy sniffed the C-4 explosive in the briefcase on the plane, she had smelled that odor many times before. She remembered its particular scent, or "signature," and knew she should sit when she smelled it.

FRAUD BUSTERS

Flo and Lucky are an amazing pair of black Labrador retrievers. They're the first animals trained to detect DVDs by their smell. Illegally copied discs are a big problem for the movie and TV industries. Dogs like Flo and Lucky identify DVDs being smuggled in luggage.

These dogs are trained to detect the smell of chemicals used to make DVDs. They can even smell the discs through several layers of plastic. The animals can't tell the difference between legal and illegal discs, so once the DVDs are located, human investigators examine them to see if they're pirated discs.

Flo is incredibly skilled at finding DVDs and CDs

Sniffer Dog at Work

Brandy was a German shepherd, but this isn't the only breed used for bomb-sniffing. Other breeds include Labrador retriever, Belgian Malinois, and vizsla (also known as a Hungarian pointer) (right). Not only are these breeds great smell detectives, but they stay calm in crowds (such as in airports) and among strangers.

Once a sniffer dog's job is done, it clears its nose with nine or ten sharp snorts, then it's ready to begin again. During a sniffer dog's career, it will often be tested and retrained to make sure its skills stay up to snuff.

DR. DOG

Dogs save lives daily. By smelling a patient's body, or a breath or urine sample, these super-sniffers can detect breast cancer, bowel cancer, and lung cancer.

Training a cancer-detection dog takes about six months. Scientists believe the dogs detect the odor of substances produced by malignant cancer cells. The canines can detect the smell of cancer almost instantly, so they can check hundreds of samples in a day, making the dogs much faster than humans.

How accurate are cancer-detection dogs? Daisy, a Labrador retriever, has sniffed cancer in more than 550 patients. She has an accuracy rate of 93 percent.

DON'T BUG ME!

Bedbugs are a problem in big cities. These insects feed on blood and get their name because they like to live in or near beds and other soft furnishings like sofas. Bedbug-detection dogs are specially trained to sniff out these pests. The canine detectives are so skilled they can identify the presence of the insects whether they're eggs, young bugs, or adults. The dogs pinpoint exactly where the bedbugs are, and that minimizes the area that needs to be sprayed with pesticides. Small dogs are chosen for this work so they can find bedbugs in crevices and gaps too narrow for humans to examine.

This puppy is checking for bombs at an airport.

Brandy's Legacy

Although airlines received many bomb threats in the late 1960s and early 1970s, Brandy's tracking down of the briefcase bomb was the first time one had actually been found on board an American jetliner.

Thanks to Brandy, a program was started in the United States to train dogs to sniff for explosives. Today, these dogs are employed in airports, railway stations, bus terminals, and at border crossings to search luggage, cargo, and vehicles for bombs and illegal items like drugs.

The National Explosives Detection Canine Team program now has about 420 teams of dogs and handlers serving in more than 75 airports and 13 mass transit systems.

CHAPTER 8

SEARCH AND RESCUE Dogs:
TERRORIST ATTACKS

Sept. 11, 2001

WHAT WAS THAT? The German shepherd froze with his tail stiff. Handler Jamie Symington knew what Trakr was telling him. The dog had caught a "live hit." There was a human lying under the piles of concrete and steel.

How was that possible? The towers had collapsed almost 24 hours ago—could someone still be alive under the rubble? Had Trakr really smelled something in all the smoke, ash, and dust?

Trakr was so insistent that Jamie called over firefighters and rescue workers. They began digging in the area the search and rescue dog had indicated. Then one of them noticed a piece of reflective fabric. Was someone really down there?

Crime-Fighting Dog

Trakr was born in the Czech Republic and was trained there as a search and rescue (SAR) dog. In 1995, when he was 14 months old, he joined the Halifax Regional Police in Nova Scotia, on Canada's East Coast. He was teamed up with James Symington, one of the founders of the canine unit for his police force. On Trakr's first day on the job, he helped make an arrest.

For six years, Trakr worked with Jamie, helping to track down more than $1 million worth of illegal goods, arrest hundreds of criminals, and find many missing people.

WOOF!

A SAR dog can rappel down mountains with its handler, climb ladders, and walk along a teetering beam in a collapsing building.

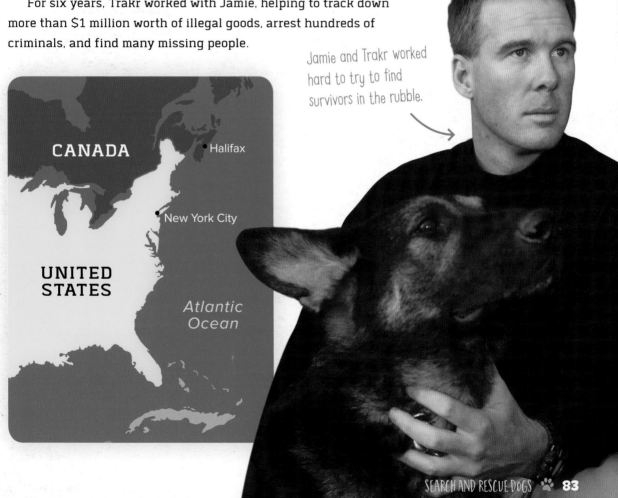

Jamie and Trakr worked hard to try to find survivors in the rubble.

CANADA

Halifax

New York City

UNITED STATES

Atlantic Ocean

TO BE A Search AND Rescue DOG

Most search and rescue dogs tend to be larger working and sporting breeds. These include Doberman pinschers, German shepherds, giant schnauzers, golden retrievers, Labrador retrievers, and rottweilers. They have longer muzzles, which helps make them better at detecting scents.

It takes up to two years to train a search and rescue dog. The dog must be agile, have great endurance, and get along with other dogs and people. The trainer, or handler, will work with the dog until it retires, usually after the four-legged rescuer has worked for about 10 years. The dog lives with the handler while they are a working team and usually after the dog retires.

Disaster Strikes

Trakr retired in May 2001. Soon after, Jamie took leave for an elbow injury and stress. On September 11, Jamie was shocked, like the rest of the world, when two planes hijacked by terrorists flew into the twin towers of the World Trade Center in New York City.

The crashes caused huge damage to both towers and started massive fires. In less than two hours, the towers had collapsed.

Smoke and ash filled the air in New York.

Jamie was glued to his television, watching the rescue operation at the site of the buildings' collapse, later known as Ground Zero. He realized he and Trakr could help, so he loaded the big dog into his car and they headed down to New York City. Trakr and Jamie drove for 15 hours straight and were on the job in New York City early in the morning of September 12.

WOOF!

A water-search dog works along the shore or in a boat to find drowning victims. The dog slaps and bites at the surface of the water where it locates a person.

"We Have a Survivor!"

Within hours of the terrorist attack, many specially trained dogs, including other German shepherds, Labrador retrievers, and even dachshunds, were on site. It was around 6:30 a.m. on September 12 that Trakr let Jamie know he'd found something in the rubble that had once been the north tower.

The workers began digging in the area Trakr had indicated. Suddenly, two of the firefighters heard a faint voice coming from deep below the pile of steel and concrete. "We have a survivor," one of the firefighters yelled.

The survivor that Trakr found was Genelle Guzman. She lay terrified below pillars and concrete. Find out more about her incredible rescue on page 89.

Mountain RESCUE DOGS

When most people think of rescue dogs working on snowy mountains, they think of Saint Bernards. These huge dogs—they weigh about 91 kilograms (200 pounds) and are about 80 centimeters (31 inches) tall—often work in groups of three. That way, if they find someone in trouble, two of the dogs can lie down beside the person to keep him or her warm. The other dog heads out and guides rescuers to the scene.

A Saint Bernard has an advantage over other mountain rescue dogs: its large, square head and big ears help it hear low, subsonic sounds (which humans can barely hear). That helps them find people trapped in avalanches. These dogs are known for being patient, smart, and easy to train.

Rescue
DOG JAKE

You might not think a dog abandoned on the streets with a dislocated hip and broken leg would have much of a future. But Jake became an SAR dog, honored for his work at Ground Zero in 2001 and after Hurricane Katrina crushed New Orleans in 2005.

This black Labrador retriever was adopted by a search and rescue team member and quickly showed that he was a good learner. He helped train younger rescue dogs, teaching them to track smells, even in the snow. The young dogs also learned from him to look up to find the scent if it was in a tree.

Tracking and Air Scenting

There are two main types of SAR dogs.

Tracking (or trailing) dogs work with their noses close to the ground. They follow a trail of human scent, no matter how rough the ground. They're following rather than searching. They start by sniffing a piece of the missing person's clothing to learn the scent, then they search for the trail. This type of SAR dog is used to find lost children or escaped prisoners and usually is on a lead held by its trainer.

Jake performs daily search and rescue exercises to stay sharp.

An air-scenting dog, also known as an area-search dog, sniffs out human scent that's in the breeze. This SAR dog works with its nose up in the air and doesn't need a piece of clothing to get started. When these dogs pick up a scent, they follow it to where the smell is strongest, where there might be a missing trekker, victims of an avalanche or mudslide, or people buried in a destroyed building.

On the site of the 9/11 disaster, it was air-scenting dogs that helped search for survivors. But there were very few, which discouraged the dogs. One of the reasons they are motivated to find live people is that they get positive feedback, which dogs crave. So handlers actually hid in the ruins of the towers and let the dogs find them so the dogs would feel successful and continue working.

Skin Rafts

Scientists estimate an SAR dog can do as much work as 20 to 30 human searchers. It's not just because it has such a keen sense of smell. Dogs also have better hearing and night vision.

Experts believe that when dogs are picking up a human scent, they're actually smelling "skin rafts." Each person loses about 40,000 skin cells every minute. These tiny cells form into flakes called skin rafts. They form a "scent cone" that a dog can easily track down because everyone's skin cells have a unique smell. The skin rafts float on air currents or may drop to the ground, depending on how the wind is moving, how humid the air is, and how hot the day is.

WOOF!

Search and rescue dogs work best at night. That's when winds tend to be calmest and skin rafts stay low. The dogs also work well in early morning and late afternoon.

A rescue dog races along on the trail of a scent.

Teamwork

German shepherds like Trakr are popular SAR dogs. They're agile, obedient, and smart. They have a double-layered coat, which keeps them warm in cold-weather searches. These dogs are big enough to pick their way over large rocks and uneven ground but small enough to be easily transported long distances to a disaster site.

SAR dogs and their handlers learn to read each other's body language. The dogs can learn about 50 words or phrases, such as "Find it," which tells the dog to begin a search, or "Show me," which the handler says when he or she wants the dog to return to where an item was found.

Working Dogs

Dogs can have many careers other than guarding, hunting, guiding, or search and rescue. Some jobs are out of this world—in 1957, a Russian mutt named Laika (right) became the first animal to orbit Earth.

The first canine movie star was Rin Tin Tin. He was a German shepherd rescued from a battlefield in World War I and went on to star in many Hollywood movies. You can still see some of them online. Other dogs perform onstage or at special events.

Hundreds of years ago, turnspit dogs ran on wheels to provide power to turn meat so it could cook over a fire or to churn butter. Dogs also used to pull small carts to deliver mail or even carry people. Herding dogs are still used to control cows and sheep. Some also herd wild geese in parks or goats being used for weed control.

Others work as cadaver dogs—they use their sniffing skills to find bodies at the scenes of disasters or accidents.

Trapped

Genelle Guzman
had been working
at the World Trade
Center (shown
here) for only nine
months, on the
sixty-fourth floor
of the north tower.
September 11, 2001,
seemed like an ordinary
morning until she heard a
deafening boom. She and
her officemates ran down
the stairs, but already Genelle
could sense the building
collapsing around her. She got
as far as the thirteenth floor
when the tower gave way.

"I felt the walls cave in,"
she remembers. "It was dark and
everything was rumbling." Genelle's
head was pinned between two
concrete pillars under the rubble.
The only thing that kept her alive
was an air pocket that allowed her
to breathe.

Rescued from the Rubble

There was no way Genelle could have known that one of the voices she heard was Jamie Symington speaking to Trakr and the other rescuers. Firefighters began digging down, around where Trakr had indicated. When they saw the reflective jacket, they moved the rubble even faster.

Trakr had been right. There was someone alive under all that concrete and steel. At 12:30 p.m., rescuers finally freed Genelle from the rubble that had trapped her for 27 hours. She was the last survivor pulled from Ground Zero.

THERAPY DOGS

Dogs can "rescue" people by comforting them when they are coping with stress, anxiety, or emotional trauma. These canines are called therapy dogs, and they provide love and reassurance to people in hospitals, retirement homes, and schools. The dogs also help people with autism. For instance, they will lie on the person to apply deep pressure, which calms and relieves stress.

After the World Trade Center attacks, as well as the attacks on the same day at the Pentagon and in Shanksville, Pennsylvania, dogs helped many people. Trained therapy dogs worked for months comforting survivors, as well as the families and friends of the victims. The dogs also helped the firefighters, police officers, and relief workers deal with overwhelming stress.

While searching the rubble left after the destruction of the World Trade Center, sometimes dogs were moved around on slings.

Trakr the Hero

There were more than 300 SAR dogs working at Ground Zero. Twenty people were pulled out alive, and the dogs also found jewelry and other items that could be returned to the victims' families.

After Genelle was dug from the rubble, Trakr worked for two more days at the site. But the conditions were terrible, and on September 14, he collapsed from inhaling too much smoke. The dog had been exposed to dangerous chemicals, his paws were burned, and he was exhausted. Trakr was treated, and then he and Jamie headed back to Halifax.

Trakr has been praised as one of history's most heroic animals. Although he died in April 2009, at the age of 15, he is still famous as the dog that found the last survivor of the 9/11 terrorist attacks.

Time Line

40,000,000
MIACIS, THE OLDEST DOG ANCESTOR, APPEARS

23,000,000
TOMARCTUS, ANOTHER DOG AND WOLF ANCESTOR, APPEARS

32,000
PEOPLE BEGIN DOMESTICATING DOGS

35,000
DOGS DIVERGE FROM WOLVES GENETICALLY

9000
THE FIRST IDENTIFIABLE DOG BREED, A GREYHOUND, APPEARS IN EGYPTIAN PAINTINGS AND CARVINGS

1914–1918
WORLD WAR I: DOGS PERFORM IMPORTANT TASKS IN THE TRENCHES AND ON BATTLEFIELDS

4000
ANCIENT BRITONS, CHINESE, EGYPTIANS, GREEKS, AND PERSIANS USE DOGS IN WAR

500
PEKINGESE BEGIN LIVING IN THE ROYAL COURT OF CHINA

456
SOTER SAVES THE CITY OF CORINTH IN GREECE

1899–1900
BOXER REBELLION IN CHINA. EMPRESS DOWAGER CIXI ORDERS PEKINGESE TO BE KILLED SO THEY DON'T FALL INTO ENEMY HANDS

CE

1
BUDDHIST RELIGION COMES TO CHINA AND PEKINGESE BECOME KNOWN AS LION DOGS

1700s
DOGS USED AS MESSENGERS IN THE SEVEN YEARS' WAR IN EUROPE

1500s
GREAT DANES AND MASTIFFS IN ARMOR FIGHT IN BATTLES

1804–1806
LEWIS AND CLARK EXPEDITION, INCLUDING SEAMAN, A NEWFOUNDLAND DOG

1925
SLED DOGS BRING
DIPHTHERIA ANTITOXIN
TO THE REMOTE TOWN
OF NOME, ALASKA

1928
MORRIS FRANK
MEETS BUDDY AND
SHE BECOMES HIS
GUIDE DOG

1929
FIRST GUIDE-DOG SCHOOL IN
THE UNITED STATES OPENS
IN NASHVILLE, TENNESSEE

1917
STUBBY AND JAMES
CONROY SAIL TO
EUROPE TO FIGHT IN
THE WAR

1939–1945
WORLD WAR II: THE K-9
CORPS GUARD AND TRACK
ENEMY SOLDIERS

1949
COMMUNIST PARTY
TAKES POWER IN CHINA
AND PEKINGESE DOGS
DISAPPEAR

1950-1953
KOREAN WAR:
AMERICAN MILITARY
DOGS ARE SHIPPED
OVERSEAS

1954-1975
VIETNAM WAR:
AMERICAN ARMY DOGS
PATROL COMPOUNDS
AND OUTPOSTS

1947–1991
DURING THE COLD WAR,
DOGS GUARD NUCLEAR
WEAPONS IN THE
UNITED STATES

1972
GERMAN SHEPHERD
BRANDY SNIFFS OUT
BOMB PLANTED ON AN
AMERICAN JETLINER

2000s
DOGS WORK WITH ARMY TO GUARD
PRISONERS, SEARCH AREAS, AND
DETECT AMBUSHES; ALSO HELP
SOLDIERS WITH POST-TRAUMATIC
STRESS DISORDER (PTSD)

2016
LUCCA BECOMES THE FIRST
UNITED STATES MARINE
CORPS DOG AWARDED THE
DICKIN MEDAL, A BRITISH
MILITARY HONOR

2001
WORLD TRADE CENTER
ATTACKED BY TERRORISTS;
SEARCH AND RESCUE DOG
TRAKR FINDS THE LAST
SURVIVOR

2011
MILITARY DOG CAIRO
HELPS CAPTURE
TERRORIST
OSAMA BIN LADEN

Seaman the Newfoundland

Fort Atkinson State Historical Park, Fort Calhoun, Nebraska

Fort Clatsop, Lewis and Clark National Historical Park, Clatsop County, Oregon

Lewis & Clark National Historic Trail Interpretive Center, Great Falls, Montana

Sioux City Lewis & Clark Interpretive Center, Sioux City, Iowa

Lion Dogs

Forbidden City (Palace Museum), Beijing, China

Natural History Museum at Tring, England

Combat Canine

National World War I Museum and Memorial, Kansas City, Missouri

Smithsonian National Museum of American History, Washington, D.C.

West Haven Veterans Museum, West Haven, Connecticut

Togo and Balto

Cleveland Metroparks Zoo, Cleveland, Ohio

Cleveland Museum of Natural History, Cleveland, Ohio

Iditarod Trail Sled Dog Race Headquarters, Wasilla, Alaska

Central Park, New York City, New York

A Real Buddy

Plaque in the Hall of Fame at the Museum of the American Printing House for the Blind, Louisville, Kentucky

Statue of Morris Frank and Buddy, Morristown Green, Morristown, New Jersey

Military Guard Dogs

Armed Forces History Museum, Largo, Florida

Museum of World War II Boston, Natick, Massachusetts

National WWII Museum, New Orleans, Louisiana

Sniffer Dog Saves the Day

American Kennel Club Museum of the Dog, St. Louis, Missouri

Merseyside Maritime Museum, Liverpool, England

Search and Rescue Dogs

National September 11 Memorial & Museum, New York City, New York

Whistler Museum, Whistler, British Columbia

MAIN SOURCES

Seaman the Newfoundland

Stephen E. Ambrose. *Lewis & Clark: Voyage of Discovery*. Washington: National Geographic Society, 2002.

John Bakeless. *The Journals of Lewis and Clark*. New York: Signet, 2004.

Isabel George. *The Dog That Saved My Life*. Bath, England: Chivers, 2010.

George S. MacDonell. *A Dog Named Gander*. 2014.

Lion Dogs

D. Caroline Coile. *Pekingese: Everything about Purchase, Care, Nutrition, Behavior, and Training*. Hauppauge, NY: Barron's, 2006.

Stanley Coren. *The Pawprints of History: Dogs and the Course of Human Events*. New York: Free Press, 2002.

Diana Preston. *The Boxer Rebellion: The Dramatic Story of China's War on Foreigners That Shook the World in the Summer of 1900*. New York: Walker Publishing Company, Inc., 2000.

David Silbey. *The Boxer Rebellion and the Great Game in China*. New York: Hill and Wang, 2012.

Combat Canine

Nigel Allsopp. *Animals in Combat*. Chatswood, NSW, Australia: New Holland Publishers, 2014.

Ann Bausum. *Sergeant Stubby: How a Stray Dog and His Best Friend Helped Win World War I and Stole the Heart of a Nation*. Washington, DC: National Geographic, 2014.

Evelyn le Chêne. *Silent Heroes: The Bravery and Devotion of Animals in War*. London: Souvenir Press, 2010.

Togo and Balto

Bob Cary. *Born to Pull: The Glory of Sled Dogs*. Minneapolis, MN: University of Minnesota Press, 2009.

Gay Salisbury. *The Cruelest Miles: The Heroic Story of Dogs and Men in a Race Against an Epidemic*. New York: W.W. Norton & Co., 2003.

Shelly Swanson. *Sled Dogs: The Breeds and Basics of Dog Sledding*. Seattle, WA: CreateSpace Independent Publishing Platform, 2015.

A Real Buddy

Stanley Coren. *How to Speak Dog: Mastering the Art of Dog–Human Communication*. New York: The Free Press, 2000.

Stanley Coren. *What Do Dogs Know?* New York: Free Press, 1997.

Peter Putnam. *Love in the Lead: The Fifty-Year Miracle of the Seeing Eye Dog*. New York: Dutton, 1979.

Military Guard Dogs

Jan Bondeson. *Amazing Dogs: A Cabinet of Canine Curiosities*. Ithaca, NY: Cornell University Press, 2011.

Nigel Cawthorne. *Canine Commandos: The Heroism, Devotion, and Sacrifice of Dogs in War*. Berkeley, CA: Ulysses Press, 2012.

Stanley Coren. *The Intelligence of Dogs: Canine Consciousness and Capabilities*. Toronto: Maxwell Macmillan Canada, 1994.

Maria Goodavage. *Soldier Dogs: The Untold Story of America's Canine Heroes*. New York: Dutton, 2012.

Sniffer Dog Saves the Day

Stanley Coren. *Understanding Your Dog for Dummies*. Hoboken, NJ: Wiley, 2007.

Stanley Coren. *Why Does My Dog Act That Way? A Complete Guide to Your Dog's Personality*. New York: Free Press, 2006.

Alexandra Horowitz. *Inside of a Dog: What Dogs See, Smell, and Know*. New York: Scribner, 2010.

Cat Warren. *What the Dog Knows: Scent, Science, and the Amazing Ways Dogs Perceive the World*. New York: Touchstone, 2015

Search and Rescue Dogs

Stanley Coren. *How Dogs Think: Understanding the Canine Mind*. New York: Free Press, 2004.

Stanley Coren. *The Modern Dog: A Joyful Exploration of How We Live with Dogs Today*. New York: Free Press, 2008.

Brian Hare. *The Genius of Dogs: How Dogs Are Smarter Than You Think*. New York: Plume, 2013.

FURTHER READING

Seaman the Newfoundland

Nick Bertozzi. *Lewis and Clark*. New York: First Second Books, 2011.

Roland Smith. *The Captain's Dog: My Journey with the Lewis and Clark Tribe*. San Diego, CA: Harcourt Children's Books, 1999.

Robyn Walker. *Sergeant Gander: A Canadian Hero*. Toronto: Natural Heritage Books, 2009.

Charlotte Wilcox. *The Newfoundland*. Mankata, MN: Capstone High/Low Books, 1999.

Lion Dogs

Lynn Bodin. *The Boxer Rebellion*. Oxford, England: Osprey Publishing, 1979.

D. Caroline Coile. *Pekingese: Everything about Purchase, Care, Nutrition, Behavior, and Training*. Hauppauge, NY: Barron's, 2006.

Jenny Drastura. *Pekingese*. TFH Publications: Neptune City, NJ, 2011.

Gene Luen Yang. *Boxers*. New York: First Second Books, 2013.

Gene Luen Yang. *Saints*. New York: First Second Books, 2013.

Combat Canine

Simon Adams. *World War I*. New York: DK Publishing, Inc., 2007.

Ann Bausum. *Stubby the War Dog: The True Story of World War I's Bravest Dog*. Washington, DC: National Geographic Children's Books, 2014.

Richard and Sally Glendinning. *Stubby, Brave Soldier Dog*. Minnetonka, MN: Olympic Marketing Corp, 1978.

Kate Klimo. *Dog Diaries #7: Stubby*. New York: Random House Books for Young Readers, 2015.

Togo and Balto

Robert J. Blake. *Togo*. New York: Philomel Books, 2002.

Pat Chargot. *The Adventures of Balto: The Untold Story of Alaska's Famous Iditarod Sled Dog*. Anchorage, AK: Publication Consultants, 2008.

Joyce Johnston. *Alaska*. Minneapolis, MN: Lerner Publications, 2002.

Elizabeth Cody Kimmel. *Balto and the Great Race*. New York: Random House, 1999.

Debbie S. Miller. *The Great Serum Race: Blazing the Iditarod Trail*. New York: Walker & Company, 2002.

A Real Buddy

Patty L. Fletcher. *Campbell's Rambles: How a Seeing Eye Dog Retrieved My Life*. Seattle, WA: CreateSpace Independent Publishing Platform, 2014.

Becky Hall. *Morris and Buddy: The Story of the First Seeing Eye Dog*. Morton Grove, IL: Albert Whitman & Co., 2007.

Eva Moore. *Buddy: The First Seeing Eye Dog*. New York: Scholastic, 1996.

Military Guard Dogs

Will Barrow. *Buster: The Military Dog Who Saved a Thousand Lives*. New York: Thomas Dunne Books, 2015.

Laurie Calkhoven. *Military Animals with Dog Tags*. New York: Scholastic, 2015.

Stanley Coren. *Why Do Dogs Have Wet Noses?* Toronto: Kids Can Press, 2006.

Peter Roop. *Tales of Famous Animals*. New York: Scholastic Reference, 2012.

Sniffer Dog Saves the Day

Nancy Castaldo. *Sniffer Dogs: How Dogs (and Their Noses) Save the World*. New York: HMH Books for Young Readers, 2014.

Dorothy Hinshaw Patent. *Super Sniffers: Dog Detectives on the Job*. New York: Bloomsbury Publishing, 2014.

Alexandra Horowitz. *Inside of a Dog: What Dogs See, Smell, and Know*. New York: Simon & Schuster Books for Young Readers, 2016.

Search and Rescue Dogs

Linda Bozzo. *Search and Rescue Dog Heroes*. Berkeley Heights, NJ: Enslow Publishers, 2010.

Donna M. Jackson. *Hero Dogs: Courageous Canines in Action*. Boston, MA: Little, Brown, 2003.

Marie-Therese Miller. *Search and Rescue Dogs*. New York: Chelsea Clubhouse, 2007.

Dale Portman. *Rescue Dogs: Crime and Rescue Canines in the Canadian Rockies*. Victoria: Heritage House Publishing, 2009.

ACKNOWLEDGMENTS

Dog my cats, but I appreciate all the work that editor Chandra Wohleber put into this book. As ever, it was a pleasure to work with her. Special thanks also to Rivka Cranley, Education and Trade Managing Editor, for all of her time, effort, and care. As well, I'm very grateful to copy editor Catherine Dorton and proofreader Mahak Jain.

I always so appreciate the creativity and dogged determination of photo researcher Sandra Booth. Thank you for such hard work on all the books we've worked on together. Many thanks to Joanna Rankin and David Montle of Pixel Hive Studio for making this book as pretty as a speckled pup.

Thanks to everyone at Annick for all of their help with this book, especially Managing Editor Katie Hearn, Marketing Manager Brigitte Waisberg, Online Marketing Manager, Brendan Ouellette. I'm a lucky dog to be able to work with such a talented group of people.

Special thanks always to my brothers, John and Douglas, and with much love and gratitude for wonderful memories of my dad. And love to Paul, the pick of the litter!

IMAGE CREDITS

odor receptors, 77, 79
Ohio River, 6, 7

Pacific Ocean, 11, 13, 63, 65, 67
pack animals, 20, 42, 55
Pakistan, 63, 71
paradogs, 70
Paris, 27, 29, 30
paws, 6, 42, 44
Pearl Harbor, 61, 63
Pekingese, 14–19, 21–25, 92, 93
Pittsburgh, Pennsylvania, 4, 5, 6
pointers, 32, 80
poodles, 19, 64
post-traumatic stress disorder (PTSD), 33, 52, 93
predators, 42
psychiatric-service dogs, 52

Rags, 30
rescue dogs, 6, 8, 31, 34, 78, 82–88, 90, 91, 93
Rin Tin Tin, 88
Rocky Mountains, 5, 6, 11
rottweilers, 84

Sacagawea, 9, 12
Saint Bernards, 85
salukis, 10
Samoyeds, 40
scent detection, 60, 63, 73, 77–79, 84, 86, 87

Seaman, 4–13, 92
search and rescue (SAR) dogs, 53, 83–88, 90, 91
Seppala, Leonhard, 40, 41, 43
serum, 38–41, 44, 46, 47
Shaktoolik, Alaska, 39, 40
shar-peis, 10
Shawnee Native people, 7
shih tzus, 10
Shoshone Indians, 9
sled dog teams, 39–41, 43–49, 93
Smithsonian Institution, 37
sniffer dogs, 72–81
sniffer-seizure dogs, 52
soldiers, 5, 11, 26, 28–35, 50, 62, 63, 65–70, 78, 93
Soter, 62, 92
St. Louis, Missouri, 5–8, 13
Stubby, 26–32, 34–37, 93
SuperDogs, 58
Switzerland, 50–53
Symington, Jamie, 82–85, 90, 91

tails, 41, 42, 44
teeth, 10, 42, 55, 64
terriers, 28–30
terrorism, 53, 71, 82, 84, 85, 91, 93
therapy dogs, 90
Tibet, 15, 22
Tibetan mastiffs, 22
Togo, 38, 40, 41, 43, 44, 49

Tomarctus, 10, 92
Topkok River, 39, 45
tracking dogs, 33, 66, 71, 74, 83, 86, 87, 93
Trakr, 82–85, 88, 90, 91, 93
tricks, 55, 58
turnspit dogs, 88

United States, 5, 6, 13, 23, 24, 28, 33, 35, 36, 48, 50–52, 59, 61–63, 65, 67, 73, 76, 81, 83, 93

vapor wakes, 69
Vietnam War, 63, 69, 93
vizslas, 80

war, 30, 31, 33, 69, 92, 93. *See also* World War I, World War II
Washington, D.C., 27, 36, 37
Wasilla, Alaska, 39, 49
wolves, 10, 11, 41, 92
World Trade Center, 53, 71, 84, 89–91, 93
World War I, 26–32, 34, 35, 37, 50, 66, 88, 92, 93
World War II, 11, 32–34, 37, 60–63, 65–68, 70, 93